Glove Puppets

Let Your Fingers Do the Talking

by Bev Gundersen

photographs by Mike Rubush

Library of Congress Catalog Card Number 89-51588
ISBN 0-87403-638-0
Copyright © 1990, Bev Gundersen
Published by The STANDARD PUBLISHING Company, Cincinnati, Ohio
A division of STANDEX INTERNATIONAL Corporation.
Printed in U.S.A.   14-03328

Contents

To the Teacher:

Setting

These glove puppets are perfect for telling Bible stories. You will literally have the whole cast of characters, and also the background scenery for an entire story, right at your fingertips. The characters and scenery are also removable, leaving you free to use the glove with all the other puppets and backgrounds in this book for numerous Bible stories.

Small children are especially attracted to these glove puppets, since they do not overwhelm them as do the larger, moving-mouth puppets. They are designed for use in a small, informal setting with the teacher and puppets in the center and the students gathered around in a circle of companionship. This relaxed setting creates a warm and friendly atmosphere where characters can step out of the Bible and become real people with the same feelings and problems that humanity still faces today.

The "little people" in this book are user-friendly and have been designed to help you carry out the important task of feeding the Lord's little lambs. **TO GOD BE THE GLORY!**

Glove Finger Puppets

These delightful glove puppets are made from an inexpensive pair of brown jersey work gloves and black velcro. Velcro comes with two sides—one side is the "hook" and the other is the "loop." Use the hook side of the velcro on the gloves and the loop side for the puppets, or vice versa. This will allow you to use the velcro on both sides and eliminate wasting half of the velcro.

The directions given may seem a bit long, but the gloves are the heart of the puppets. You only have to make these gloves once, so a little extra time spent on them now to do them properly as the directions below state, will pay off later!

As they will get a great deal of use, you may also want to use a fabric protector such as Scotchguard (3M Company) to protect them from soil.

Materials for one glove:
10 inches of 3/4 inch wide, black velcro
2 inches of 2 inch wide, black velcro. Since this width is not always available you may substitute two 2 inch long strips of 3/4 inch wide and sew these side by side to make one wide strip 2 inches x 1 1/2 inches.

Cut 3/4 inch wide black velcro for the gloves as follows:
Pinky finger—1 3/4 inches
Ring finger—2 inches
Middle finger—2 inches
Pointer finger—2 inches
Thumb—1 1/2 inches

The black velcro blends in easily with the brown glove and does not distract from the puppets themselves. Slightly round off the corners of the velcro pieces so that there will be no sharp edges to catch and pull off the gloves. These pieces of velcro will be *sewn on the back of each finger* by hand. Beginning at the tips of the fingers, sew the velcro on with overcast stitching using heavy carpet thread. Position the thumb velcro so it is located slightly over the inside seam towards fingers.

Sew the 2 inch length of 2 inch wide black velcro to the *back of the hand* of the glove so that it is slightly forward of the middle of the glove and about 3/8 of an inch above the cuff.

Your glove is now ready to use. By fastening the puppets on the back of the glove, you can fold the fingers out of sight that are not being used. This glove is so large and easily manipulated that a child can slip it on his hand, so the figures are facing him, and tell himself the story.

As some fingers are easier to move than others, place the puppets as indicated so that the primary characters are on the pointer, pinky, and thumb positions. Those puppets which are secondary, or need to move together, are placed on the ring and middle fingers which work together.

General Directions

A glue gun works well for the large pieces, but a thick, white glue is better for the smaller pieces. For details such as eyes, use a tiny amount of glue and apply with a toothpick.

1. Glue the velcro pieces on the body backs first unless otherwise specified.
2. Glue the robe on body front. Unless directed otherwise, use robe #1 for all adult puppets and child robe for all child puppets. If the cloth, which is used for some pieces, tends to ravel use a substance such as "Fray Check" to treat material.
3. Add trim to robe, sleeves, hands, etc.
4. Glue pom-pom on head circle, being sure to glue pom-pom down at robe neckline.
5. Many of the faces have a nose. This is indicated by a solid line showing where to make a tiny slit. Cut this slit open and make the nose by gluing a narrow line where the pattern shows a dotted line. Press this together to form nose, tapering it to nothing at top of forehead.

   The men's faces show this dotted nose line but because they have no lower face there is no slit line. In these faces glue the nose as shown by the dotted line on pattern. Press this together to form nose, tapering to nothing at top of forehead.

   Face #11 and Goliath also have a mouth slit. This is done to add an "upper lip" to some of the characters or as for Goliath—insertion of teeth.
6. Glue the face to front of head pom-pom, leaving "beard," "mustache" or "hair" sticking out where desired. Female puppet faces are glued to robe at chin so no pom sticks out. Pull a few strands of pom-pom over top of all faces and glue down to cover forehead.
7. Add eyes, and any head trims—hat, cap, scarf, headband, etc.

8. A touch of blush has been added to the cheeks of female puppets to help distinguish them from their male counterparts.
9. For puppets using only pom-pom heads, a small felt circle is added to the back of the pom-pom to strengthen it. This circle should be the same color as the pom-pom.
10. Scenery usually is double thickness to add strength to pieces. Single thicknesses of felt disintegrate after prolonged use with velcro.

For trims use old buttons, jewelry pieces, and/or sequins. Here is the perfect place to use up odds and ends of these plus small scraps of brightly colored felt and fabric. Flesh, tan, or light pink felt may be used for skin colors. Other colors listed are only suggestions. Use a permanent ink marker to add details to felt pieces where directed. All velcro is 3/4 inch width unless specifically stated differently.

For simplification purposes we will refer to pom-poms as "poms." The hair colors are not true to ethnic groups but have been chosen to help young children differentiate between the various characters in the stories.

Eyes are made with black half-round pieces or beads which can be purchased at craft stores. Half-rounds are flat on the bottom and attach easier than beads. In this book, we have used the term "eyes" for either half rounds or beads.

Puppet Plays

Each play uses the glove puppets and a familiar Bible story. The glove is worn so that the puppets are on the *back* of the teacher's hand. Place each character on the appropriate finger before class time. Those puppets not in immediate use are kept folded down into the palm of the hand to keep them out of sight. As the characters are facing you and at the tip of your fingers, it becomes a simple matter to keep track of each character. Directions for raising, lowering, adding, or removing characters and props are shown in parentheses in each drama. A simple smock or apron can provide a large pocket where extra puppets or backgrounds can be kept until needed. By using a dark colored smock and holding the glove in front of it, you provide a suitable background which will help your students to concentrate on the puppets and the story they illustrate.

Sing It Again

Suitable words about the story are sung to an old, well-known tune in this section of each chapter. By using new words to an already familiar melody, the songs are easy to learn and reinforce the lesson.

Fingerplay

This section of each chapter uses motions and rhyme to further strengthen the story. By utilizing body and mind, the truths of each lesson become ingrained in the children's learning. Directions for the movements are given in parentheses.

In the Beginning

Genesis 2:7—3:24

(Adam, Eve, raccoon, fox, serpent, angel)

Adam *(middle)*
1 1 1/2" black pom
2 5 MM eyes
face #5
flesh, green felt
1 1/2" velcro
Add bush #1 to cover lower body.

Eve *(pinky)*
1 1 1/2" brown pom
2 5 MM eyes
face #7
flesh, green felt
3 small artificial flowers
2" velcro
Glue flowers on bush #2 at x's. Fasten bush to cover lower body. Add flower to hair. Blush the cheeks.

Raccoon *(ring)*
1 1 1/2" brown pom
1 1/2" white pom

1 1" white pom
3 5 MM eyes
white, black, brown felt
1" velcro
Cut 1 1/2" white pom in half. Cut it flat and trim to a figure 8 shape. Glue to head pom to form cheeks. Make mask by using face #3 and fringing it in towards eyes at center. Attach this mask over the cheeks. Trim the 1" white pom like a cone for muzzle and fasten to bottom edge of mask. Use 1 eye as nose. Cut the slit in ears #1 and lap to form dart. Add ears to sides of head. (If cut pom falls apart, apply a mixture of white glue and water to it after face is completed. Allow to dry.)

Fox *(ring)*
1 1 1/2" red-brown pom
2 1/4" white poms
1 1/8" white pom
3 5 MM eyes
rust felt
1" velcro
Glue the two 1/4" and the 1/8" poms together on head to create muzzle. Cover with nose top and bottom. Fasten other half of the 1 1/2" white pom from raccoon to create cheeks. Lap ears #2 over at bottom slit and sides before gluing to sides of head. Use 1 eye for nose. If desired, whiskers of black carpet thread may be added by knotting thread on each side of muzzle to hold in place.

Snake *(thumb)*
6 1/2" yellow-green poms
2 5 MM eyes
yellow-green felt
1 1/2" velcro (cut in half lengthwise)
Trim one pom into a point at one end to fit head shape. Glue 4 poms to felt body. Trim tail pom into an oval with point at one end.

Angel (*pointer*)

1   1 1/2" yellow pom
2   5 MM eyes
face #10
flesh, white, yellow, orange felt
gold trim
2" velcro

Glue sleeve trim to *back* side of sleeves robe #2 and hands #1 to *front* side of sleeves so when they are glued together they are in the correct places. Trim neck and bottom of robe. Make flaming sword by fastening yellow sword #1 on top of orange sword #2. Fasten hands around sword.

Garden of Eden (*hand*)

green, brown, red, white felt
2" velcro

Fasten tree top #1 to trunk #1. Fringe grass #1 and attach to trunk. Attach fruit to tree at x's and bird at dot. Add details to bird with marker.

Puppet Play

Narrator: God made a beautiful world according to His plan. It had heavenly lights, land, water, plants, and all kinds of animals. But something was missing. God was lonely. He wanted to have someone very special whom He could love and talk to and who would love and talk to Him in return. So God made a man. He named the man Adam. (*Adam up*) God made a beautiful garden home for Adam. It was more beautiful than any park or garden we can see today. It was called Eden. In it, birds sang in the trees, flowers bloomed, and animals strolled through the grass. God let Adam take care of Eden and enjoy its beauty. In return, He asked Adam to obey Him in only one thing. God planted a test tree in the middle of the garden and told Adam he must not eat the fruit of that tree. (*Add tree*) "If you ever eat fruit from that tree, you will die!" God warned him. And soon God noticed that Adam was lonely too. He needed someone to help him take care of the garden. Perhaps one of the animals could be his helper. So God brought all the animals and birds to Adam and let him name them.

Adam: (*Fox and raccoon up*) I will name you fox. And you, little masked friend, shall be called raccoon.

Narrator: But none of the animals were right for Adam. He needed a helper like himself. So God made a woman and gave her to Adam for his wife. (*Eve up*)

Adam: Thank you, God, for this woman. I will name her Eve.

Narrator: Adam and Eve were very happy living in Eden. They enjoyed everything there. They loved each other. And in the evenings, when all was quiet and cool in the garden, they walked and talked with God Himself. You wouldn't think anything could happen to spoil their wonderful life together, would you? But it did. For Adam and Eve were not the only ones in the world. Satan, God's enemy, was there too. And it was Satan, in the form of a snake, who spoiled everything God had planned for Adam and Eve. (*Snake up*) One day the snake came to talk to Eve.

Snake: Did God really say that you must not eat fruit from any tree in the garden?

Eve: Oh no. God told us we could eat from all of the trees except the one that is in the middle of the garden. If we eat its fruit, we will die.

Narrator: Then Satan told the first lie.

Snake: You won't die. If you eat the fruit from that tree you will learn about good and evil. Then you will be like God! You want to be like God, don't you? Then you could talk better with Him and understand Him more. He would like that.

Narrator: Eve should have stopped listening to the snake and gone away. But instead she went to the test tree in the middle of the garden. The fruit on it did look beautiful. And she did want to please God. So Eve took some of the fruit and ate it. She took some of it to Adam.

Eve: Here, Adam, eat this fruit and we will be like God.

Narrator: As soon as Adam and Eve ate the fruit, a terrible thing happened. Instead of becoming like God, for the first time in their lives, they were afraid. When God came to visit with them that evening, they were so afraid they hid from Him. But of course, you can never hide from God. He knew what had happened and called to them, "Where are you?"

Adam: I was afraid of You and I hid.

Narrator: God was heartbroken. He asked Adam, "Did you eat fruit from that tree? I commanded you not to eat from that tree." Adam and Eve did just what we often do. They blamed someone else for their disobedience.

Adam: It was Eve's fault. She gave it to me.

Eve: It was the snake's fault for tricking me.

Narrator: God was very sad. Now He would have to punish Adam and Eve for disobeying Him. But first He punished the snake. "You will have to crawl on your stomach and eat dust all your life." (*Down snake*) Then God sent Adam and Eve out of their beautiful garden home. (*Down fox and raccoon*) Now Adam would have to work hard to make the plants grow. There would be weeds and thorns growing along with the good plants. God put an angel at the entrance to the garden. (*Angel up*) He gave the angel a fiery sword to keep Adam and Eve from going back into the garden. God still loved Adam and Eve and He gave them a wonderful promise. "Someday I will send a Savior to take the punishment for your sin. If you trust in Him, you will live forever with Me in a heavenly home." God kept His promise and sent His Son, the Lord Jesus, to be that Savior. If we trust in Jesus, then we too, like Adam and Eve, will live forever with God in His heavenly home.

Adam and Eve in God's Garden

(tune: "The More We Get Together"/"Did You Ever See a Lassie?")

Did you ever see a garden, a garden, a garden;
Did you ever see a garden like the one that God made?

It had flowers, trees, and bushes, and grasses and fruit;
It had animals, all kinds—this garden God made.

God made Adam and Eve, to live in the garden.
To enjoy all that He made and love God always.

But they listened to Satan and disobeyed God;
Then God promised them a Savior—Christ Jesus the Lord.

God's Garden

God planted a garden
  (*Finger "plants" seed in other hand.*)
So lovely and bright.
He gave it clear water,
  (*Move fingers to indicate rippling water.*)
And lots of sunlight.
  (*Make arch over heads with arms.*)
Fruit grew on the trees.
Flowers bloomed everywhere.
  (*Cup hands.*)
Animals slept in the shade.
  (*Lay heads on hands.*)
Birds flew through the air.
  (*Thumbs together; wave hands to indicate motion of wings.*)
Fish swam in the water.
  (*Place one hand over other, wiggle thumbs to indicate swimming.*)
Stars twinkled at night.
  (*Snap fingers over head.*)
God looked at it all
  (*Place hand above eyes.*)
And said, "It's just right."
  (*Nod head.*)

High and Dry

Genesis 6:9—9:17

(Noah, man, boy, two rabbits, sheep, monkeys)

Noah (*pointer*)
1   1 1/2" white pom
2   5 MM eyes
face #2
flesh felt; striped material
miniature carpenter tool or gray felt to make one
2" velcro
Attach #1 hands inside sleeves of robe #2. Fasten hands around miniature tool.

Man (*thumb*)
1   1 1/2" black pom
2   5 MM eyes
face #15
tan, black, teal felt
1" velcro
Cut a long, thin strip of teal felt and tie around head for headband.
Glue in place.

Boy (*thumb*)

1   1 1/2" gold pom
2   4 MM eyes
face #10
flesh, gold felt
1/8" blue ribbon
1" velcro
Use ribbon for headband.

Rabbits (*pinky*)
2   1 1/2" gray poms
4   1/4" white poms
4   5 MM eyes
pink, gray felt
2   1" pieces velcro
Glue white poms for cheeks and add felt nose. Glue inner ear #3 to ear back #4 and attach to top of head pom.

Sheep (*ring*)
2   1 1/2" white poms
2   1/2" black poms
4   5 MM eyes
black felt
pink embroidery floss
2   1" pieces velcro
Glue black pom for nose. Dip floss into white glue. Let dry and add to nose to indicate nostrils and mouth. Attach ears #6.

Monkeys (*middle*)
2   1 1/2" brown poms
2   3/4" brown poms
4   5 MM eyes
tan felt
2   1" pieces velcro
Attach small brown pom for lower face. Cut slit and glue a narrow line on jaw and lap over to make small dart. Join jaw and face at dotted line. Glue this combined muzzle piece over the small pom to create face. Add ears #5.

Ark *(hand)*
tan, red felt
1 3/4" velcro
Glue ark to back and attach roof. Add details on ark with marker.

Rainbow *(hand)*
red, yellow, green, blue felt
1 3/4" velcro
Beginning with red, fasten each color band to back. Overlap each smaller band. Fasten velcro where shown.

Puppet Play

Narrator: A long time after Adam and Eve had to leave the beautiful Garden of Eden, the earth was filled with people. They were the children and grandchildren of Adam and Eve, but these people didn't love God or want to obey Him. They only cared about themselves. God felt very sad. He decided to destroy all those selfish people. Only one man and his family loved and obeyed God. That man was named Noah. *(Noah up)* Because Noah loved Him, God wanted to save his life. One day while Noah was talking to Him in prayer, God told Noah about His plan. "Noah."

Noah: Yes, God. I am here.

Narrator: "I am going to send a great flood to destroy all the evil people on earth. I want you to build a big boat. You must follow my directions, because you and your family must live in the boat. You will be the only people left alive."

Noah: I will do everything You command me, Lord.

Narrator: Soon Noah was hard at work on the big boat. His neighbors came by to watch him. *(Man and boy up)*

Man: What are you building, Noah? I've never seen anything like it.

Noah: It's a boat. I'm going to call it an ark.

Boy: What's a boat?

Noah: It's sort of a house that will float on water.

Man: What water? Why there's no water for many miles around here.

Noah: Maybe not now, but God is going to send a great flood and then there will be water everywhere.

Boy: Why is God going to send a flood?

Noah: He is going to destroy all the evil people with it. Everyone who doesn't love or obey Him will drown in the flood. But there's still time for you to tell God you're sorry for your sin. Maybe He will save you, too.

Boy: Why is the boat so big?

Noah: That's so it can hold all the animals.

Man: What animals?

Noah: God told me to bring two of every kind of bird, animal, and crawling thing on board the ark.

Man: You mean you are going to live with animals?

Noah: Yes. God told me to bring a mother and father of every kind on board the ark. And I will even have seven of some kinds of them.

Boy: How are you going to get them?

Noah: God said they will come to me.

Man: I've heard enough foolishness. Come, let's leave this crazy man alone. *(Man and boy down)*

Narrator: Despite his neighbors' insults, Noah kept busy building the ark. Weeks, months, and years went by. Every day he sawed, and pounded, and hoisted boards to make the ark bigger. At last the ark was finished. *(Add ark)* Then, just as God had said, the animals came to Noah. There were monkeys, swinging from tree to tree. *(Monkeys up)* And sheep came baaing across the fields. *(Sheep up)* Even little rabbits came hop, hopping to the ark. *(Rabbits up)* Noah and his family gathered food for all the animals and stored it along with their own food on the ark. Then God spoke to him again. "Noah."

Noah: Yes, Lord, I'm listening.

Narrator: "It's time to go into the ark." So Noah and all his family went into the ark. God shut the big door behind them. For seven days nothing happened. Then they heard it—the patter of raindrops on the roof. Soon the patter became a roar. It was as if God opened the windows of heaven and poured out great waterfalls of rain. At the same time the lakes and rivers bubbled up with great fountains of water from below. For forty days and nights the rain continued. Noah's neighbors had climbed hills and mountains until the water covered everything. Then Noah couldn't see the top of even the tallest mountain. The whole earth was covered with water. And on top of it all, the ark gently rocked back and forth. Inside, Noah and his family were busy taking care of all the animals and keeping the ark clean. For many months Noah and his family lived in the ark. Then God sent a strong wind to dry up the water. The water went down until the ark settled on the top of a mountain. Still Noah waited until God told him to come out. At last that day came. "Noah."

Noah: Yes, Lord.

Narrator: "It's time for you and your family to come out of the boat. Bring every animal out with you." How glad Noah was to be on dry land again. To show God how thankful he was, Noah built an altar.

Noah: Thank you, God, for saving me and my family.

Narrator: God made a promise to Noah. "I will never destroy the earth again with a flood. I am putting my rainbow in the clouds as a sign to you." *(Remove ark; add rainbow)* Now, whenever we see the rainbow, like a bridge of beautiful colors in the sky, we can remember that God *always* keeps His promises.

Noah Built An Ark

(tune: "Old MacDonald Had a Farm")

Father Noah built an ark. Praise, praise the Lord.
And on this ark he had two kittens. Praise, praise the Lord.
With a meow-meow here, and a meow-meow there,
Here a meow, there a meow, everywhere a meow-meow.
Father Noah built an ark. Praise, praise the Lord.

(This song can be made longer by using different animals and sounds.)

Noah's Ark

God told Noah to build an ark
   (Pound fists on each other.)
For it was going to rain.
   (Wiggle fingers downward.)
Animals came to fill the ark,
Hurrying down the lane.
   (Move fingers quickly in palm of other hand to indicate running.)
God shut the ark's big door.
   (Clap hands.)
And kept them safe inside.
   (Finger in palm of other hand; close hand around finger.)
When the land was dry again,
   (Extend hands to sides; palms up.)
Noah thanked God for the ride.
   (Fold hands; bow head.)

The Last Laugh

Genesis 17:15-19; 18:1-16; 21:1-7

(Abraham, Sarah, two angels, the Lord, Baby Isaac)

Abraham (pointer)
1   1 1/2" white pom
2   5 MM eyes
face #2
flesh, red felt
fancy trim
2" velcro
Glue sleeve trim to *back* side of sleeves robe #2 and hands #1 to *front* side of sleeves so when they are glued together they are in the correct places. Trim bottom edge of robe. Glue only a small spot on the lower edge of each sleeve to robe, leaving the rest free.

Sarah (thumb)
1   1 1/2" white pom
2   5 MM eyes
face #11
flesh, light blue felt
striped material
silver and gold trim

1 3/4" velcro
Trim yoke #1 and robe as shown. This face has an extra cut for mouth. Glue face to head pom being sure to leave the top lip free to add facial expression. Pleat headscarf #2 around head. Blush the cheeks lightly as Sarah is an old woman.

Lord (middle)
1   1 1/2" tan pom
2   5 MM eyes
face #2
flesh, white felt; striped material
gold trim
1 1/2" velcro
Fasten coat #2 to robe and add gold trim.

Angels (ring and pinky)
2   1 1/2" yellow poms
4   5 MM eyes
faces #10
flesh, white felt
gold rickrack and braid
2   2" velcro pieces
Glue rickrack to bottom edge of robes and add belts cut from braid.

Baby Isaac (Sarah)
1   1/4" black pom
face #1
flesh, white felt
1 1/4" *hook* side velcro
Fold and glue baby blanket #1 into a wrapped baby shape. Attach pom to blanket. Add eyes using marker. The hook velcro will attach to Sarah and baby can be added at proper place in story.

Tent (hand)
tan, brown, green felt
1 3/4" velcro
Cut 2 pieces of tent. Fasten tree top #2 to

trunk #2 and attach to side of tent at x's. Add details with marker.

Puppet Play

Narrator: Abraham was God's friend. *(Abraham up)* Abraham promised God he would serve Him all his life. And God promised Abraham he would have as many children as the stars in the sky. There was just one problem. Abraham and his wife Sarah *(Sarah up)* didn't have *any* children. No, not even one. But Abraham trusted God and believed He would keep His promise. Many years passed and Abraham and Sarah still did not have any children. Even more time went by until Abraham was a very old man. Then one day when Abraham was praying, the Lord repeated His promise, "I will give you and Sarah a son." Abraham laughed when he heard this.

Abraham: I trust you, Lord, but I am 100 years old and Sarah is 90. We're too old to have children.

Narrator: It seemed impossible, but Abraham knew he could trust God. Then one day Abraham got a surprise. It was noon and he was sitting in the shade of his tent. *(Add tent)* Suddenly he saw three men coming toward him. He could see they were different from his neighbors. *(Lord and angels up)* Abraham hurried to meet them.

Abraham: You must have come from very far away. Here, friends, sit down under this tree. I'll bring some water so all of you can wash your feet. Then I will bring you something to eat.

Lord: That is fine. Do as you said.

Narrator: The men sat down in the shade. Abraham told Sarah to make some bread. Then he hurried to where the cattle were and picked out a fat calf. A servant cooked it and soon Abraham was back with dinner for his guests. He gave them meat, bread, butter, and milk. Now Abraham could tell that these three men were very unusual. And indeed they were. Two of them were angels and the third one was the Lord. What a special way for God to visit His friend Abraham! Abraham stood nearby the men to serve them. When they had finished eating, the Lord spoke to him.

Lord: Where is your wife, Sarah?

Abraham: She's there, in the tent.

Lord: I will return about a year from now and Sarah will have a son.

Narrator: Now Sarah was listening inside the tent. When she heard the Lord say this, she laughed to herself.

Sarah: Abraham and I are too old to have a baby.

Narrator: The Lord knew that Sarah had laughed.

Lord: Why did Sarah laugh? Doesn't she trust the Lord? Nothing is too hard for Him to do. Yes, a year from now you and Sarah will have a baby boy.

Narrator: Then the men left. *(Lord and angels down)* Inside the tent, Sarah had stopped laughing. She was thinking about what the Lord had said.

Sarah: No, nothing is too hard for God. Now He has even told us *when* He will give us a son. I will trust the Lord to keep His word.

Narrator: Time seemed to pass quickly after the special visitors had left. The weeks turned into months and the Lord cared for Sarah just as He had said. At exactly the right time, everything happened as God had said it would. Abraham and Sarah had a beautiful baby boy. *(Add Baby Isaac to Sarah)*.

Sarah: How thankful we can be to God for our little son!

Abraham: We will name him Isaac. Isaac means laughter.

Sarah: Yes, God has made us laugh with joy. And everyone who hears about Isaac will be happy and laugh with us.

Abraham: I'm so glad we trusted God to keep His promise.

Narrator: Yes, God turned Abraham and Sarah's laughs of wonder into laughs of joy. Abraham's family grew and grew in number until they became a great nation. Today we call them the Jews or Israelis. Like Abraham, we can trust God to keep His promises. And when we trust Him, the Lord gives us joyful laughter too.

Sarah's Lullaby

(tune: "Brahms Lullaby")

Lullaby, and goodnight,
 Baby Isaac, sleep tight.
God has given you to me
 And I rock you tenderly.

You are mine, baby boy,
 And you've brought me such joy.
How I praise God above
 Who gave me this child to love.

Baby Isaac

This is baby Isaac
 (Hold up finger.)
Who brought his parents joy.
 (Hold up three fingers.)
God, our heavenly Father,
 (Point upward.)
Gave them this baby boy.
Mother Sarah held him tight
 (Finger in palm of other hand; close hand around finger.)
Her heart was filled with love.
 (Cross hands over heart.)
Baby Isaac slept and dreamed,
 (Lay head on hands.)
Watched by God above.
 (Place hand above eyes.)

Cradled in the Lap of Luxury

Exodus 1:11—2:10

(Jochebed, Miriam, Princess, Servant, Baby Moses)

Baby Moses *(pinky)*
1 1/2" brown pom
face #1
miniature basket (about 1" diameter)
flesh, white, green felt
1" velcro
Fold blanket #2 where indicated and glue loosely. Attach inside basket to give impression of body wrapped in it. Glue face to pom. Add eyes using marker. Fasten pom to blanket and basket. Glue small clumps of grass #2, #3, #4, and #5 around basket.

Mother Jochebed *(thumb)*
1 1 1/2" brown pom
2 5 MM eyes
face #6
flesh, light blue felt; striped material
2" velcro
Glue headscarf #2 to head and pleat it around face. Blush the cheeks.

Miriam *(pointer)*
1 1" brown pom
2 4 MM eyes
face #8, child body
flesh, medium felt; striped material
1 3/4" velcro
Add headscarf #1 to head and pleat around face. Blush the cheeks.

Egyptian Princess *(middle)*
1 1 1/2" black pom
2 5 MM eyes
face #7
1 jewelry three-ring crown
2 jewelry filigree or sequins
flesh, white, light green, black felt
gold loop trim
2" velcro
Attach yoke #1 to robe and trim yoke. Add trim to drape #1 and glue on robe where indicated. Cut eyelashes of felt and glue in place. Decorate head with band, filigree, and crown. Cut 2 tiny pieces of loop trim and glue to each side of face for earrings. Blush the cheeks.

Servant *(ring)*
1 1 1/2" brown pom
2 5 MM eyes
face #5
flesh, white felt
gold trim
1/8" green ribbon
2" velcro
Trim robe. Add ribbon headband to pom. Blush the cheeks.

Nile River *(hand)*
green, blue, light blue felt
2" velcro
Fringe grass #6 to dotted line. Add water #1 and #2.

Puppet Play

Narrator: Abraham's family had become a great nation. They were called the Hebrews or Israelites and lived in Egypt. Life was very hard for them there. The king of Egypt was afraid because there were more Hebrews than Egyptians, so he made them his slaves. He forced them to make bricks for his many building projects. But the harder they worked, the stronger they became. Then the king made a terrible law. All the baby boys born to the Hebrews were to be thrown into the river. There they would either drown or be eaten by the crocodiles. What a cruel king he was! Now one of the Hebrew women, who was named Jochebed, *(Jochebed up)* had a baby boy. He was a beautiful baby, full of dimples, smiles, and coos. Mother Jochebed loved her little son very much. For three months she hid him from the Egyptians. But the baby grew quickly and it became harder to hide him every day.

Miriam: *(Miriam up)* Mother, I was playing outside and I could hear the baby laughing. I was afraid the Egyptians would hear him too! Shouldn't we do something about it?

Jochebed: Yes, Miriam. I am afraid you are right. The time has come when I can't keep him quiet anymore.

Miriam: What shall we do, Mother?

Jochebed: I have been praying about it and the Lord has given me a plan. You can help me with it. First you must go to the river. Gather the biggest, strongest reeds that grow there and bring them to me.

Narrator: Miriam loved her little brother and quickly obeyed her mother. She hurried to gather the hollow reeds that grew along the riverbank. *(Add Nile River)*

Miriam: Here are the reeds, but how will they save the baby's life?

Jochebed: Watch and see, Daughter. You keep the baby quiet while I work.

Narrator: Miriam rocked the baby while her mother wove the reeds into a beautiful basket.

Jochebed: There, that should be big enough to hold the baby. Now, Miriam, fill this container with tar. I will needs lots of it.

Narrator: Soon Miriam was back with the tar. With wide eyes she watched her mother cover the inside and outside of the basket with it. Then Jochebed let the basket dry in the sunshine. When it was finished it was . . .

Miriam: A little boat! It can float on the water and anything inside it will stay dry.

Jochebed: Yes, Miriam, it is a boat. And we will place the baby inside it.

Miriam: But how is a boat going to save the baby's life?

Jochebed: Now comes the most important part of the plan. I am going to hide this boat in the grass along the riverbank.

Miriam: But won't the Egyptians still hear the baby and find him?

Jochebed: That is just what will happen, Miriam. But the Lord has shown me that He has chosen one special Egyptian to find our baby. Come, let's put some blankets into the basket. Then we will put the baby in it and take him to the river.

Narrator: Mother Jochebed carefully carried the basket to the river. *(Baby Moses up)* She hid it in the tall weeds. There it bobbed up and down, rocking the baby to sleep.

Jochebed: Miriam, you must be very brave. Stay here and guard the baby. Watch what happens. And remember, the Lord will take care of him. *(Jochebed down)*

Narrator: Miriam didn't have long to wait.

Soon the daughter of the Egyptian king and some of her servants came to the river to take a bath. The princess saw the little boat in the tall grass. (Princess and servant up)

Princess: What can be inside the basket? Bring it to me so I can see what it is.

Servant: Here is the basket. Do you think it is a treasure or someone's lunch?

Narrator: The princess opened the basket and saw the baby boy.

Princess: Why, he's crying. He must be frightened, poor baby.

Servant: Whose baby can it be?

Princess: This is one of the Hebrew babies.

Narrator: Miriam had been watching all that happened. She hurried to the princess and bowed.

Miriam: Would you like me to find a Hebrew woman to take care of him for you?

Princess: Yes, please.

Narrator: Miriam ran all the way home and was soon back with her mother. (Jochebed up) The princess knew that this woman and little girl cared a great deal about the baby. Perhaps she realized he was part of their family.

Princess: Take the baby and care for him. I will pay you.

Narrator: So Miriam and Jochebed took the baby boy back home with them. (Princess and servant down)

Miriam: You were right, Mother. God did have a special plan for our baby.

Narrator: No one would bother the baby now, for everyone learned that he had been adopted by the princess as her own son. She named him Moses which meant "pulled out," because she pulled him out of the river. He grew up to be one of the most important people in the world. You are important to God too and he has a special plan for your life. Just let Him tell you about it.

The Basket Bed

(tune: "Jingle Bells")

Up and down,
Up and down,
 Baby Moses ride.
Floating in the basket bed,
 You are safe inside.
Up and down,
Up and down,
 Sister watches near.
Mother prays to God the Lord,
 Knowing He will hear.

Baby Moses

See upon the River Nile,
 (Hand above eyes.)
Moses in his basket small.
 (Finger in palm of other hand; close hand around finger.)
Placed there by his mother's hands;
 (Extend hands; palms up.)
Floating near the reeds so tall.
 (Hands over head.)
Sister Miriam hides close by
 (Crouch down to indicate hiding.)
While the Princess and her maid
Hear a cry and go to look
 (Cup hand around ear.)
Where the little child is laid.
 (Finger in palm of other hand; close hand around finger.)
Up comes the cover of the basket
 (Open hand; reveal finger in palm.)
The princess sees the little boy
 (Hold up finger.)
"I will keep him as my own."
 (Point to self.)
Moses is safe now; oh what joy!
 (Clap hands.)

On the Level

Joshua 5:13—6:20

(Joshua, priest, soldier, wall)

Joshua *(pointer)*
1 1 1/2" black pom
2 5 MM eyes
face #2
flesh, brown, gray, green, orange felt
gold sequin
2" velcro
Glue belt #2 to robe and add sword #3 at x.
Attach drape #2 to robe front and cloak #2
to side back of robe. Add details to drape,
cloak and sword with marker. Trim drape at
shoulder with sequin.

Priest *(thumb)*
1 1 1/2" brown pom
2 5 MM eyes
face #15
flesh, white, blue, brown felt
1" velcro
Priests wore special clothing in specific colors so the directions here should be followed
exactly. Attach face high on pom and do *not*

extend strands over forehead for hair. Trim
pom so top is quite narrow above face.
Gather white cap so it stands tall and
spreads out. Attach to top of pom. Cover
with blue hat band #2.

Soldier *(thumb)*
1 1 1/2" gold pom
2 5 MM eyes
face #2
flesh, gold, blue felt
1" velcro
Glue headband around head.

Wall *(middle, ring, and pinky)*
tan felt
2 2" velcro
1 1 3/4" velcro
Add details with marker and attach people
at x's. Fasten velcro strips to each tower
section for these three fingers.

Man *(wall)*
1 1/2" black pom
flesh felt
face #17
Add eyes using marker. Attach pom to wall
at x.

Woman *(wall)*
1 1/2" brown pom
flesh felt
face #1
Add eyes using marker. Blush cheeks.
Attach pom to wall at xx.

Sign *(hand)*
gray, tan, brown, blue felt
1 1/2" velcro *hook* side
2" velcro
Glue sign front to back where indicated.
Fasten sign to post where shown. Attach

bird to sign. Glue rocks to bottom of post. Glue 2" velcro to back side of rocks. Secure the *hook* velcro to the back of sign crosspiece. This hook side will adhere to the glove material to help hold it in place. Add details to sign, bird, and rocks with marker.

Puppet Play

Narrator: After a very long time as slaves, God used Moses to lead His people, the Israelites, out of Egypt. They spent many years in the wilderness. Now God had chosen Joshua *(Joshua up)* to lead the Israelites into the land He had promised to Abraham. The people already living in this promised land were wicked and fierce. They would not give up the land without a fight. One of the hardest cities to take would be Jericho. *(Add Jericho sign)* The people in Jericho had built two great walls around their city. These walls were very, very tall. Houses were built on top of them and held the two walls together. *(Wall up)* The people inside the town had shut and locked their gates to keep the Israelites out. One morning Joshua went out to look at the city. He wondered how God's people would be able to tear the great walls down and take the city. Then a wonderful thing happened. Joshua met a man who gave him a plan to get inside Jericho. This man was the same man who had visited Abraham and promised him a son. Do you know who the man was? Yes, He was the Lord. Now the Lord promised Joshua that if the Israelites obeyed Him they would have victory over Jericho. Joshua hurried back to his camp to tell the Israelites about the plan. *(Priest and soldier up)*

Joshua: The Lord says for six days we are to march around the city of Jericho. Each day we will march around it one time. The priests are to march behind the soldiers. No one is to say a word.

Soldier: The priests? What good will they be? They don't know how to fight.

Joshua: They will carry the Holy Box of God.

Priest: Is that all we will be doing—marching and carrying the Holy Box?

Joshua: No, you priests will also blow your trumpets while you march.

Soldier: I don't know. That sounds like a crazy way to get inside the city.

Joshua: On the seventh day we will march around the city seven times. Don't say a word until I tell you. Then shout!

Priest: Are you sure this plan will work?

Joshua: Yes, I am sure. The Lord gave me this plan. He has promised that if we obey Him, He will give us victory over Jericho. Now let's get ready and march around the city. Remember, don't say a word until I tell you.

Narrator: So the Israelite soldiers and priests marched around the city one time. Then they went back to their camp. Early the next morning they marched around the city again. Soldiers led the parade. The priests followed them. They carried the Holy Box and blew their trumpets. They marched one time around Jericho. Then Joshua led them back to their camp. The people inside Jericho watched everything and wondered what it meant.

Woman: Have you seen those men marching around our city?

Man: Yes. Why do you think they are acting so strange?

Woman: I don't know. Maybe they are trying to frighten us.

Man: Humph! Well they don't scare me. They look silly out there.

Woman: Perhaps they are going to attack us. I'm afraid.

Man: If they think they can take our city by

simply marching around it they are wrong! I'm just going to ignore them.

Narrator: Every day for six days Joshua led the army and priests around Jericho one time. No one spoke a word. The only sound was the trumpet blasts by the priests. The people inside the huge walls couldn't understand such actions. Then came day seven. Joshua got up at dawn and led the Israelites around the city. One. Two. Three. Four. Five. Six. Seven times they marched around Jericho. Then Joshua gave the command:

Joshua: Now, shout! The Lord has given you this city!

Narrator: The army shouted. They shouted so loudly that the people inside the walls had to cover their ears. They shouted so loudly that the ground shook beneath their feet. At the same time, the priests blew their trumpets. They blew until their faces were red and their eyes bugged out. Then it happened. At first there was only a crack in the corner by the gate. Then the crack spread up and across the outer wall. The wall began to shake and shiver. *(Wiggle wall)* So did the people inside it. Then with a great roar, the walls fell down. Flat! *(Wall down)* Joshua led the army straight into Jericho and they conquered the city. God had a plan. Joshua didn't understand it, but he knew he could trust the Lord. We can trust God's plans too. Even when we don't understand them.

The Fall of Jericho

(tune: "The Mulberry Bush")

The Israelites marched around Jericho,
　　Jericho, Jericho;
The Israelites marched around Jericho
　　Six days in a row.

The priests blew their horns but nobody spoke,
　　Nobody spoke, nobody spoke;
The priests blew their horns but nobody spoke
　　For six days in a row.

On the seventh day they marched seven times,
Marched seven times, marched seven times;
The priests blew their horns and the soldiers
　　cheered;
And the walls came tumbling down.

God's Plan

Jericho's walls were very tall.
　　(Hands over head.)
How could the Jews get inside?
　　(Shake head.)
Joshua prayed to the Lord for help.
　　(Fold hands; bow head.)
God gave a plan to guide.
　　(Point upward.)
Priests blew horns while the people marched
　　(Move fingers to indicate marching.)
Six days around the town.
　　(Hold up six fingers.)
The seventh day they marched seven times,
　　(Hold up seven fingers.)
Blew horns and shouted. The walls fell down!
　　(Clap hands.)

Out of the Mouths of Babes

1 Samuel 1:9-20, 24-28; 3:1-10, 19-21

(Baby Samuel, Boy Samuel, Hannah, Elkanah, Eli, Shekinah Light)

Baby Samuel *(Hannah)*
Use Baby Isaac from story "The Last Laugh."
Attach to Hannah at proper place in story.

Boy Samuel *(pointer)*
1   1" brown pom
2   4 MM eyes
face #8, child body
flesh, blue felt; striped material
1 1/2" velcro
Glue coat #3 over robe.

Hannah *(thumb)*
1   1 1/2" black pom
2   5 MM eyes
face #7
flesh, pink, rose felt
1 1/2" velcro
Add belt #1 to robe. Fold and glue headscarf
#2 around face. Blush the cheeks.

Elkanah *(middle)*

1   1 1/2" brown pom
2   5 MM eyes
face #3
flesh, green, dark green felt
2" velcro
Add belt #1 to robe. Attach headband
around pom.

Eli *(pinky)*
1   1 1/2" white pom
2   5 MM eyes
face #13
flesh, white, blue, golden-yellow felt
1/8" blue ribbon
gold braid; 2 silver sequins
1 3/4" velcro

As this puppet is the high priest, be sure to
follow color directions. God was very specific
as to just what the high priest was to wear!
We have tried to adhere as closely to the
Biblical description as possible, adapting it
to puppet size. Attach blue coat #2 to white
robe. Trim bottom of coat with gold trim.
Apply yellow ephod over coat and add
checkered lines and ties with marker. The
breastplate is also yellow and has 12 lines
to indicate the precious stones which sym-
bolized the 12 tribes. Use ribbon for belt
and sash and sequins for engraved shoulder
stones. The headdress is made of hat crown
#2 and hat band #2. Apply ribbon in a cross
shape as shown on pattern and gather hat
crown. Trim pom to almost cone shape
above face. Fasten hat crown to top of head.
Glue band around head being sure to fasten
to bottom of hat crown, face, and hair. Apply
a small oblong piece of gold braid over forehead where shown.

Shekinah Light *(ring)*
white, yellow, gold felt

gold glitter

1 1/2" velcro

Glue a white light #1 to yellow #2. Fasten these pieces to gold #3 back. Spread a thin coat of white glue over this combined piece. Sprinkle on glitter. Let dry and shake off excess glitter. To protect other puppets from glitter, wrap this piece separately before storing.

Tabernacle *(hand)*

tan felt

Cut two pieces from tabernacle pattern. Add details to front with marker. Glue to back piece.

Puppet Play

Narrator: An Israelite man named Elkanah *(Elkanah up)* took his family and went to worship the Lord in Shiloh every year. Now Elkanah had two wives. One of them had several children and Elkanah gave special gifts to her and her children when they went to Shiloh. The other wife, Hannah, *(Hannah up)* had no children. She would feel bad every year when Elkanah gave these gifts to his family.

Elkanah: Don't feel bad, Hannah. You know I love you very much.

Hannah: I am glad, my husband, but I still wish we had a child. *(Elkanah down)*

Narrator: One year while they were in Shiloh, Hannah went to God's house to pray. She was so sad that she cried as she prayed. Her lips moved, but she was praying only in her heart.

Hannah: Lord, if You will give me a son, I will give him back to You to serve You all his life.

Narrator: Eli, the high priest, *(Eli up)* was sitting at the door to God's house. He saw Hannah's lips move, but couldn't hear her voice.

Eli: What are you doing, Woman? Are you drunk or being foolish?

Hannah: No, Master. I'm talking to the Lord because I am so sad. I was telling Him my problem.

Eli: Then may He give you what you asked of Him. Go home now in peace. *(Eli down)*

Narrator: Hannah went home. She didn't cry anymore. Now, she was happy, for she believed the Lord would answer her prayer. Indeed He did, for in less than a year God gave Hannah and Elkanah a baby boy. *(Add Baby Samuel to Hannah)*

Hannah: I will name you Samuel, which means "Asked of God," because I asked the Lord for a son and He has given you to me. *(Remove Baby Samuel)*

Narrator: Hannah loved her baby. She fed him, played with him, and sang to him as she rocked him to sleep. But Hannah also remembered her promise to God. When little Samuel *(Boy Samuel up)* was old enough to leave her, she took him to Shiloh. There she brought him to Eli *(Eli up)* in God's House.

Hannah: Do you remember me, Master? God answered my prayer and gave me this little boy. Now I give him back to the Lord. *(Hannah down)*

Narrator: Eli knew this pleased God. He let Samuel live in God's house. He taught him how to pray and read God's Word. And Samuel helped Eli every way he could. He ran errands, filled the oil lamps, and polished the containers in God's house. One night when Samuel was in bed, God called him. *(Shekinah Light up)* "Samuel." Samuel got up and ran to Eli, thinking he had called.

Samuel: Here I am. You called me.

Eli: I didn't call you. Go lie down.

Narrator: Samuel went back to bed. Before very long, the Lord called again. "Samuel." Samuel hurried to Eli.

Samuel: I am here. You called me.

Eli: I didn't call you. Go back to bed.

Narrator: Again Samuel went back to bed. A third time the Lord called, "Samuel." Once more the little boy scurried to Eli.

Samuel: Here I am. You called me.

Narrator: Then Eli realized the Lord was calling Samuel.

Eli: Go lie down. If He calls again, say, "Speak Lord. I am your servant. I am listening."

Narrator: Samuel went and lay down. The Lord came and stood nearby. "Samuel." Samuel sat straight up in bed. Could it really be the Lord God who was calling him? Shivers ran down Samuel's back and the little hairs on the back of his neck stood up. He felt tingly all over. He answered bravely.

Samuel: Speak, Lord. I am your servant. I am listening.

Narrator: Then the Lord gave Samuel a message for Eli. *(Shekinah Light down)* That was the beginning of a wonderful friendship between Samuel and God. Samuel listened closely whenever the Lord spoke to him. The Lord was with the boy as he grew up and all the Israelites knew Samuel was God's messenger. We can listen for God's messages to us through His Word. And we can be His willing helpers just like Samuel.

Helpers and Listeners

(tune: "Twinkle, Twinkle Little Star")

Little Samuel loved the Lord
And he helped Him every day.
In the Lord's House where he lived
Obeying Eli in every way.
I can be a helper too;
Just like Samuel, kind and true.

Little Samuel heard the Lord
As he lay in bed one night;
Quickly answered, "Here am I,
Your servant who will do what's right."
I can be a listener too,
Just like Samuel, and so can you.

Little Samuel

In the temple in Jerusalem
    (Clasp hands; raise pointer fingers.)
There lived a little boy.
    (Hold up finger.)
Samuel helped the priest Eli
    (Extend hands.)
And filled his life with joy.
    (Draw smile on face with finger; smile.)
One night the Lord called out "Samuel,"
    (Cup hands around mouth.)
While the little boy was asleep.
    (Lay head on hands.)
Samuel answered, "Here I am;"
    (Point to self.)
Your word I'll always keep."
    (Extend hands together; palms up to indicate holding Bible.)

The Bigger They Come, the Harder They Fall

1 Samuel 17:1-52

(David, Goliath, King Saul, Eliab, Abinadab)

David *(pinky)*
1   1" brown pom
2   4 MM eyes
face #10, child body
flesh, brown, red felt
1/8" yellow ribbon
black floss
1 small pebble
1 1/2" velcro
Attach hands #2 to sleeves and glue sleeves to child's robe at shoulders. Glue ribbon headband around pom. Add pebble to sling at x. Thread floss through hands, through sling at dots and back through hands. Fasten securely.

Goliath *(pointer)*
1   2" black pom
2   6 MM eyes
face #14, Goliath body
tan, brown, red, white, gold felt
black floss

2" velcro
Glue robe to armor. Fringe sash and attach to robe. Add belt #3. Glue shoulder pads #2 to robe where indicated. Apply pads #1 over these. On this puppet glue nose together all the way to top of forehead. This makes Goliath look mean! Insert teeth and glue to mouth before adding to head pom. Dip floss in white glue and allow to dry. This will be used for mustache. Attach to face at x.

King Saul *(thumb)*
1   1 1/2" gray pom
2   5 MM eyes
face #2
flesh, purple felt; striped material
gold braid trim, sequin, bead, large jewelry
bell cap
1 3/4" velcro
Do not glue velcro to body first! Glue robe to body. Trim cloak #1 with braid. Fasten robed body inside cloak, turning cloak down over robe as indicated. Attach velcro to back of cloak. Add sequin and gold braid "chain." Glue bell cap to pom top. Add bead to center to complete crown.

Eliab—Oldest Brother *(middle)*
1   1 1/2" red-brown pom
2   5 MM eyes
face #2
flesh, teal, yellow felt
black braid trim
polyester stuffing
2" velcro
Attach coat #2 to robe and trim. Gather hat crown #1 where shown. Stuff lightly with polyester to round out as if head is inside. Glue to top of pom. Fasten hat band #1 around head being sure to fasten to hat crown and pom.

Abinadab—Older Brother *(ring)*
  1 1 1/2" yellow pom
  2 5 MM eyes
  face #5
  flesh, green, orange felt
  2" velcro
  Add belt #1 to robe. Gather cap and glue over head pom and puppet back body.

Stream *(hand)*
  light blue felt
  6 small pebbles
  1 1/2" *hook* velcro
  1 1 3/4" velcro
  Cut two pieces of stream pattern. Attach pebbles to front at x's. Glue to back piece. Attach short *hook* velcro above longer strip on back. This hook side will adhere to glove and help hold stream in place.

Puppet Play

Narrator: The Israelites and Philistines were at war. The Philistines had a champion fighter named Goliath. *(Goliath up)* Goliath was big. Goliath was HUGE! Why if one Israelite soldier stood on the shoulders of another, they would still not be as tall as Goliath! Even the coat of armor he wore for protection weighed as many pounds as a woman. And Goliath was mean. Goliath was WICKED! Every day, when the two armies lined up to fight, he stepped out in front of the Philistines and shouted out curses against the Israelites.

Goliath: Choose just one man to fight with me. If he can kill me, the Philistines will become your servants. If I kill him, you must become our servants. Come on, I dare you! Send one of your men to fight me.

Narrator: King Saul and the Israelites were very afraid of Goliath. No one would fight him. Then one day an Israelite named Jesse sent for his son David, who was in the fields taking care of the sheep. *(David up)* Jesse told David to take some bread to his brothers who were in Saul's army. He also sent a gift of cheese to their commander. Then

Jesse asked David to bring back some word from his brothers. David left early the next morning. He got to the valley where the two armies were, just as they were lining up for battle. He quickly delivered the food and ran to find his brothers, Eliab and Abinadab. *(Eliab and Abinadab up)* While David was talking to his brothers, Goliath came out. He shouted curses against the Israelites as usual. The Israelites were very afraid and ran away from him.

David: Who was that?

Eliab: That was Goliath the Philistine. Every day he taunts us like this.

David: Why do you let him get away with it?

Abinadab: Didn't you see how big he is? Who would dare fight with him?

David: But he's a Philistine. He mocking the Lord. Why does he think he can speak against the armies of the living God like that?

Eliab: You're only a boy. Do you think you are better than King Saul and the men in this army? Why did you come here anyway? Why aren't you home taking care of the sheep? You just came to see us fight and now you're acting like you could take on Goliath and beat him.

Abinadab: Why don't you go back home, David? You're going to get us in trouble talking like that! *(Eliab and Abinadab down)*

Narrator: But many of the other soldiers had also heard David talking to his brothers. They hurried to King Saul and told him what David had said.

King Saul: *(King Saul up)* Bring David to me.

Narrator: Soon David was standing before King Saul in his tent.

David: Don't be discouraged. I, your servant,

will go and fight this Philistine giant!

Narrator: King Saul was taller than any of the other Israelite soldiers. David was only a little shepherd boy. But Saul knew that if someone didn't volunteer to fight Goliath, he would have to fight the giant himself.

King Saul: How can you fight a warrior like Goliath?

David: I killed a lion and a bear when they attacked my sheep. Goliath is against the armies of the living God. The Lord saved me from the lion and the bear, and I know He will also save me from this Philistine.

King Saul: Go then, and may the Lord be with you. *(King Saul down)*

Narrator: King Saul gave David his armor and weapons, but David wasn't used to them. He couldn't even walk around in them. David took off the armor and laid aside the weapons. Then he ran down to a nearby stream and chose five smooth stones. *(Add stream)* David took the stones and his sling and went to meet Goliath. *(Goliath up)*

Narrator: Goliath was furious when he saw David. Because David was only a boy, Goliath thought the Israelites were making fun of him.

Goliath: Come here. I'll feed your body to the birds of the air and the wild animals.

David: I come to you in the name of the Lord of heaven's armies and the God of Israel. You have spoken out against Him. But today the Lord will give you to me. I'll kill you, and cut off your head! Then all the world will know there is a God in Israel. The Lord alone will save His people.

Narrator: With an angry roar, Goliath rushed to attack him. David raced to meet him. He took one of the stones and put it in his sling. He twirled it around. Then he let it go. Up, up, up flew the stone with a whirring sound.

THURWACK! It struck Goliath on his forehead. With a groan of disbelief he tottered forward. Down, down, down he fell. CLUNK! The earth shook and the giant lay face down on the ground. David dashed to him, took Goliath's own sword and cut off the giant's head. God gave the Israelites a great victory over their enemies that day. God will give us victory over our enemies too when we trust in Him to help us. Like David, we might be small, but we have a great God.

David's Sling

(tune: "Mary Had a Little Lamb")

David had a little sling, little sling, little sling.
David had a little sling, to protect his sheep.

Goliath was a giant tall, giant tall, giant tall.
Goliath was a giant tall, but he mocked the Lord.

David prayed and used his sling, used his sling, used his sling.
David prayed and used his sling to kill this wicked man.

Brave David

Goliath was big.
    (Hand over head.)
A very bad man,
    (Draw turned down mouth on face with finger; look angry.)
He spoke against God
    (Point upward.)
And the Israelites ran.
    (Move fingers quickly in palm of other hand to indicate running.)
David prayed
    (Fold hands; bow head.)
And used his sling
    (Swing arm over head; throw to indicate releasing stone.)
To kill the giant.
He did a brave thing!
    (Clap hands.)

Go Jump in the River

2 Kings 5:1-17

(Naaman, Wife, Servant Girl, Elisha, Servant)

Naaman (*middle*)
    1 1 1/2" black pom
    2 5 MM eyes
    face #16
    tan, red, white felt
    gold trim; jewelry—gold filigree or sequin
    2" velcro
Do not glue velcro to body first! Glue robe to body. Trim cloak #1 and robe. Fasten robed body inside cloak, turning cloak down over robe as indicated. Attach velcro to back of cloak. Add filigree to robe.

Wife (*pointer*)
    1 1 1/2" red-brown pom
    2 5 MM eyes
    face #7
    flesh, teal, white felt
    gold loop trim; jewelry—gold filigree or sequin
    2" velcro
Trim neck and bottom of robe. Fasten drape

#1 to robe and trim drape. Glue filigree to shoulder of drape. Attach headband of loop trim. Cut 2 tiny pieces of loop trim and glue to each side of face for earrings. Blush the cheeks.

Servant Girl (*thumb*)
    1 1" brown pom
    2 4 MM eyes
    face #8, child body
    flesh, pink felt
    1/8" pink ribbon
    1 1/2" velcro
Use ribbon for belt. Double ribbon over and glue at side of belt for tie ends. Use ribbon for headband.

Elijah (*pinky*)
    1 1 1/2" gray pom
    2 5 MM eyes
    face #3
    flesh, lavender felt; striped material
    1 3/4" velcro
Cut striped material crosswise and use for belt and headband.

Servant (*ring*)
    1 1 1/2" tan pom
    2 5 MM eyes
    face #15
    flesh, green felt; striped material
    narrow white braid
    2" velcro
Add coat #2 to robe. Trim V-neck and bottom of coat with braid. Fasten felt headband around pom, fastening it at side of head with a small piece, extending loose.

Jordan River (*hand*)
    blue, green felt
    2" velcro
Cut two pieces of river pattern. Add grass

clumps #'s 2, 3, 4, and 5 to front piece at dots. Attach to back piece.

Puppet Play

Narrator: The Syrians lived north of Israel. These people didn't know or love the Lord. They worshiped a god named Rimmon. The Syrians often made raids into Israel and stole things. On one trip, they stole a little Israelite girl and brought her back with them as a servant. *(Girl up)* The little girl missed her family and home, but she grew to love her kind master, Naaman, and his wife. *(Naaman and Wife up)* She tried very hard to help them. She must have prayed for them too. Soon Naaman and his wife also came to love the little girl. Naaman was an officer in the Syrian army. He was strong and brave, but he had a harmful skin disease called leprosy. The little girl felt sad about Naaman's sickness. One day she talked to her mistress about it.

Girl: I wish that Master Naaman would go to the Lord's prophet in Israel. He could heal my master of his disease. *(Girl down)*

Wife: My husband, the little Israelite girl thinks you should go to Israel for healing. *(Wife down)*

Narrator: Naaman told his friend, the king of Syria, about it. The king loved Naaman and wrote a letter to the king of Israel. He thought the king of Israel could command the prophet to heal Naaman. Soon Naaman was on his way to Israel. He took along a gift of clothing and money to give the king there. When the king of Israel read the letter from the king of Syria, he was very upset. He knew he could not heal Naaman of his disease. Only God could do that. The king was afraid Syria was only trying to make trouble for Israel. If the king had loved the Lord, he would have sent Naaman to Elisha, the Lord's prophet. But the king worshiped idols instead of the living God. Elisha, the man of God, heard how upset the king was. He sent him a message. *(Elisha up)*

Elisha: Send Naaman to me. Then he will know there is a messenger of God in Israel.

Narrator: Naaman hurried to Elisha's house. But Elisha didn't come out and talk to him. Instead he sent a message by his servant.

Elisha: Tell Naaman to go to the Jordan River. He is to wash in it seven times and he will be healed. *(Elisha down)*

Narrator: Naaman was very angry because Elisha hadn't come out to talk to him personally.

Naaman: Let's go home! Elisha didn't come see me. He didn't call on his God or even wave his hand over me to heal me. The Jordan River is dirty and muddy. If I only need to wash seven times in a river, I'll go home and wash in one of our own rivers.

Narrator: One of Naaman's servants came to talk to him. *(Servant up)*

Servant: Master, you would have done something hard if the prophet had asked you. He only asked you to wash seven times in a nearby river. That is such an easy thing to do. Won't you just try it and do as Elisha asked?

Narrator: Then Naaman realized how foolish he had been.

Naaman: Turn around. We will go back to the Jordan River. *(Add River)*

Narrator: One. Two. Three. Four. Five. Six. Seven times Naaman washed in the Jordan River. The servants held their breath. Would their master be healed as the prophet had said? Then wonder of wonders—Naaman gave a whoop of joy.

Naaman: The disease has disappeared entirely! My skin is clean. It is as clear as when I was a little boy.

Narrator: Naaman and his servants were so glad that they danced around in a circle.

Naaman: Come on, everybody. Let's go thank Elisha.

Narrator: What a happy parade they made back to the prophet's house. This time Elisha came out to meet them. *(Elisha up)*

Naaman: Now I know that the only God in all the earth is the Lord of Israel. Please take this gift of clothes and money from me.

Elisha: No. I will not accept it. I serve the Lord. You can't buy healing from Him.

Naaman: From now on I won't make any offerings or sacrifices to any other god. I'll only worship the Lord. *(Elisha down)*

Narrator: Naaman returned home healthy and very happy. The little servant girl must have been happy too. Now her master had not only been healed, but he loved and worshiped the living God. We can also tell others about the Lord. And when we do, He will use us to bless them.

The Little Girl's Message

(tune: "Reuben, Reuben, I've Been Thinking")

"Naaman, Naaman I've been thinking
If you went to Israel

There the prophet of the Lord could
Make you clean and well again."

Naaman, Naaman went to Israel
Heard the prophet of the Lord
Washed seven times in Jordan's waters
Was made clean and well again.

Naaman Is Healed

Naaman was a soldier brave,
   (Flex arm to show muscle.)
But he was sick indeed.
Then his slave girl told him about
   (Cup hands around mouth.)
A prophet who'd meet his need.
   (Nod head.)

"Go wash, seven times," Elisha said,
   (Hold up seven fingers.)
"In Jordan's waters deep.
   (Hold hands apart to indicate depth.)
Your skin will be healed and you will be clean
   (Point to others.)
The Lord this promise will keep."
   (Point upward.)

Naaman did as he was told.
   (Move hand up and down to indicate dipping in river.)
It was a simple thing.
God healed him as Elisha said.
   (Nod head.)
And Naaman praised God the king.
   (Clap hands.)

If I Were King

2 Chronicles 22:10—23:21

(Queen Athaliah, Jehoida, Jehosheba, Joash, 2 priests/temple guards)

Queen Athaliah *(thumb)*
1   1 1/2" brown pom
2   5 MM eyes
face #11
flesh, red, pink, white felt
1 jewelry bell cap
gold trim; sequin
black embroidery floss
1 3/4" velcro
Glue yoke #2 to robe. Trim robe at yoke and bottom of skirt. Apply drape #2 and add fold lines with marker. Fasten sequin to shoulder drape. This face has an extra cut for mouth. Glue face to head pom being sure to leave the top lip free to add facial expression. Dip floss in white glue and allow to dry. This will be used for eyebrows. Attach a short v-shaped piece of floss on nose between eyes. Fasten bell cap on head for crown. Blush the cheeks.

Uncle Jehoida *(middle)*

1   1 1/2" black pom
2   5 MM eyes
face #2
flesh, blue, white, golden-yellow felt
gold trim; 2 silver sequins
1/8" blue ribbon
2" velcro
Jehoida was high priest so his robe is identical to Eli's in "Out of the Mouths of Babes."

Aunt Jehosheba *(pointer)*
1   1 1/2" black pom
2   5 MM eyes
face #5
flesh, pink, lavender felt
2" velcro
Glue belt #3 to robe. Attach one end of headscarf #2 to side of face. Wrap around head and secure scarf at other side of face and over shoulder. Add headband. Blush the cheeks.

Joash *(ring)*
1   1" black pom
2   4 MM eyes
face #9, child body
flesh felt; striped material
narrow gold braid
1 jewelry bell cap
1 1/2" velcro
1/2" *hook* velcro
Use braid for belt. Double braid over and glue at side of belt for tie ends. Headband is made of braid. Attach *hook* velcro to bell cap. This crown can be added to Joash at proper time in story.

Temple Guards *(pinky)*
Man #1
1   1 1/2" gold pom
2   5 MM eyes

face #15
flesh, white, blue, gold felt
1" velcro
Priests wore special clothing in specific colors so the directions here should be followed exactly. Attach face high on pom and do *not* extend strands over forehead for hair. Trim pom so top is quite narrow above face. Gather white cap so it stands tall and spreads out. Attach to top of pom. Cover with blue hat band #2.

Man #2 *(pinky)*
Use priest from story "On the Level."

Temple *(hand)*
white felt
2" velcro
Cut two pieces of temple pattern. Add details to front with marker.
Glue to back piece.

Puppet Play

Narrator: Athaliah *(Athaliah up)* was a wicked woman. She never went to worship the Lord in the beautiful temple near her home. *(Add temple)* Instead she worshiped false gods and coaxed her son, the king, to do the same thing. When he was killed by an enemy, Athaliah planned to do a very evil thing. She would kill all his family. Just imagine a grandmother doing such a thing to all her grandchildren! Then she could rule the land all by herself. But the Lord knew all about wicked Athaliah and He had a plan to stop her. It included the king's sister Jehosheba *(Jehosheba up)* and her husband, the high priest Jehoida. *(Jehoida up)* The plan all started just before Athaliah carried out her sinful deed. *(Athaliah down)*

Jehoida: We must do something to stop Athaliah from ruling the Israelites. If she becomes the queen, they will start to worship false gods.

Jehosheba: Yes, she has already caused many of the king's family to worship her idols. But there is one baby boy that she hasn't controlled. His name is Joash. I am going to help him and his nurse escape from her.

Narrator: Jehosheba was true to her word. She took baby Joash and his nurse and hid them in a bedroom of her home. When Athaliah ordered all the king's family to be murdered, little Joash and his nurse were safe inside the temple of the Lord. But the baby would have to be protected for many years to come.

Jehosheba: I wish that we could let Joash crawl around and explore the house more.

Jehoida: We can't take any chances of Athaliah seeing him. You'll have to keep him out of sight.

Narrator: Soon little Joash learned to walk and talk.

Jehosheba: Couldn't we find just one other little boy for Joash to play with?

Jehoida: I'm sorry my dear. We must keep him hidden. He can't grow up like other children. It is hard, I know, but it is the best we can do. If his grandmother were to find him, she would kill him. *(Jehoida down)*

Narrator: Aunt Jehosheba tried to make life happy for the little boy. She often played games with him. Each night she tucked him in bed and heard his prayers. *(Joash up)*

Joash: Thank you God for the sunshine today. Bless Uncle Jehoida and Aunt Jehosheba and my nurse. Amen.

Jehosheba: Haven't you forgotten something, Joash?

Joash: I don't think so—oh yes! And please, God, forgive me for pulling the puppy's tail. Amen. *(Jehosheba down)*

Narrator: When Joash grew old enough, his uncle taught him to read and memorize God's Word. *(Jehoida up)*

Jehoida: Try to say it again, Joash. Just try.

Joash: "I am the Lord your God. You must not . . . must not have any other . . .

Jehoida: Must not have any other what? Think about what you are saying, Joash.

Joash: "I am the Lord your God. You must not have any other gods except me. You must not make for yourselves any idols." What's an idol, Uncle?

Jehoida: It is any false god, Joash. Many of the people around us worship statues made of wood, stone, and metal. These statues cannot hear when the people pray to them. They cannot answer prayers and they are not alive like the Lord. Remember, Joash, you are to worship Him only.

Narrator: At last, when Joash was seven years old, his uncle decided it was time to do something about Athaliah. He called together the temple guards and the leaders of the people. *(Guards up)*

Jehoida: The Lord promised King David that his family would continue to rule the Israelites. One of the king's sons is still alive. It is time we made him king and stopped Queen Athaliah from leading the people. Now, here is what I want you to do . . .

Narrator: All the temple guards and the people did everything the High Priest commanded. They took spears and shields and stood around the altar and the temple. Then Jehoida brought out Joash.

Jehoida: Here is Joash. He is the rightful king.

Narrator: Then Jehoida poured olive oil on Joash's head.

Guard #1: Put the crown on his head! *(Add crown)*

Narrator: Jehoida gave Joash a copy of God's Law and appointed him king over all of God's people.

Guard #2: Long live King Joash!

Narrator: Queen Athaliah soon heard all the shouting. She ran to the temple to find out what was happening. *(Athaliah up)*

Athaliah: What is going on here?

Jehoida: Capture her! Take her outside the temple and kill her like she murdered the king's family.

Narrator: That day the people agreed to be the Lord's special people. They tore down the temple and idols of the false gods and once again worshiped the Lord. They brought Joash into the palace and placed him on the throne. What a wonderful day that was. Yes, God can keep us safe from trouble, just as He kept little Joash safe.

Joash

(tune: "Mary Had a Little Lamb")

Joash was a little boy,
Little boy, little boy.
Joash was a little boy
Who became the king.

He repaired the Lord's temple,
Lord's temple, Lord's temple.
He repaired the Lord's temple
So all could worship there.

Joash Becomes King

When he was only seven years old
    (Hold up seven fingers.)
His uncle brought him out.
    (Hold finger up high.)
The people made Joash king that day.
    (Hold hands in circle above head to indicate crown.)
"Long live the King!" arose their shouts.
    (Hands around mouth.)

It's Not the Heat, It's the Humility

Daniel 3:1-30

(Shadrach, Meshach, Abednego, King Nebuchadnezzar, 2 Babylonians)

Shadrach *(pointer)*
1   1 1/2" black pom
2   5 MM eyes
face #2
flesh, teal felt
Metallic braid
2" velcro
Trim hem and V-neck with braid. Use braid for belt. Fasten braid around pom for headband.

Meshach *(middle)*
1   1 1/2" brown pom
2   5 MM eyes
face #3
flesh, gold, light blue felt
gold braid and trim
2" velcro
Glue drape #2 to robe. Apply trim to cloak #2 at guidelines. Fasten cloak to side back. Use braid as headband.

Abednego *(ring)*
1   1 1/2" yellow pom
2   5 MM eyes
face #16
flesh, green, purple felt; striped material
black loop trim
2" velcro
Glue yoke #1 and drape #3 to robe. Glue trim to curved edge of drape. Attach belt over drape and robe.

Nebuchadnezzar *(pinky)*
1   1 1/2" gray pom
2   5 MM eyes
face #13
tan, cerise, white felt
gold trim; sequins; small jewelry bead cap and 3-ring crown
1 3/4" velcro
Do not glue velcro to body first! Glue robe to body. Trim cloak #1 with braid. Fasten robed body inside cloak, turning cloak down over robe as indicated. Attach velcro to back of cloak. Add sequins to robe. Glue bead cap into 3-ring crown. Glue this entire crown to head.

Man #1 *(thumb)*
1   1 1/2" black pom
2   5 MM eyes
face #15
tan felt
1/4" beige ribbon
1" velcro
Use ribbon for headband.

Man #2 *(thumb)*
1   1 1/2" brown pom
2   5 MM eyes
face #13
tan felt
1/8" yellow ribbon

1" velcro
Use ribbon for headband.

Oven *(hand)*
gray, red, black, orange, yellow felt
2" velcro
Glue red interior to oven as shown. Attach black coals to interior where indicated. Cut orange and yellow flames. Add flames to oven as pictured.

Puppet Play

Narrator: The Babylonians captured the Israelites and carried many of them back to Babylon. Three young boys: Hananiah; Mishael; and Azariah; were among the captives. The king of Babylon gave these boys the Babylonian names of Shadrach, Meshach, and Abednego. They were trained for three years to serve the king. When they had completed their training, he made them officers in his government. It was hard for these young men to continue serving the Lord in a land where the people worshiped false gods. But Shadrach, Meshach, and Abednego loved the Lord and promised to serve Him only. This became harder when the king built a huge statue of his god. The statue was 90 feet high and 9 feet wide and was covered with gold. It stood on a great level area where it could be seen for many miles. Then one day the king called together all the important men in his government. *(King Nebuchadnezzar up)* They stood in front of the giant statue.

King Nebuchadnezzar: All of you are to obey my command. When you hear the music of my musicians you must bow down and worship the golden statue. It is my god. Anyone who doesn't worship it will be quickly thrown into a fiery furnace!

Narrator: The men looked around them. At one side of the statue was an oven that was used to bake bricks. An enormous fire was blazing in it. Thick black smoke poured out the chimney and flames leaped out of the door. *(Add oven)* The men could feel the heat from this furnace on their faces. Their knees began to shake with fear. The musicians began to play. Immediately the men fell on their faces before the statue. Not one of them wanted to end up in that fiery furnace. But wait! What was this? Not everyone was bowing to the idol. Three men were still standing! *(Shadrach, Meshach, Abednego up)* Yes, Shadrach, Meshach, and Abednego stood tall and brave in the middle of all the fearful worshipers of the golden statue. Some of the Babylonians had been very jealous of these Israelites. *(Man #1 and Man #2 up)* When they saw them refuse to bow to the idol, the men hurried to tell the king.

Man #1: Oh great King Nebuchadnezzar. We heard your command to bow down and worship the gold statue. When the music began, we obeyed. But there are some men of Judah who didn't obey your command.

Man #2: They don't worship your statue or serve your god. Shouldn't they be thrown into the fiery furnace, oh mighty king?

King Nebuchadnezzar: Who are these men?

Man #1: Their names are Shadrach, Meshach, and Abednego. You made them officers in your government.

King Nebuchadnezzar: Bring them to me at once! *(Man #1 and Man #2 down)*

Narrator: Soon the three Israelites stood before the king.

King Nebuchadnezzar: Is it true that you don't serve my gods? Didn't you worship the gold statue when you heard the music? Didn't you understand? I will give you another chance. But this time you *must* do what I have commanded. If you do not, you will be thrown into the blazing furnace. Then no god will be able to save you from my power!

Shadrach: Yes, oh king, you can throw us into the furnace for not obeying you.

Meshach: Our God, the Lord, can save us from you and your punishment. We will praise Him if He does this.

Abednego: But even if the Lord doesn't save us, we won't serve your gods. We refuse to worship your gold statue!

King Nebuchadnezzar: That's enough! Heat up the oven seven times hotter than before. Call my strongest soldiers. Have them tie up Shradrach, Meshach, and Abednego and throw them into the blazing furnace!

Narrator: So the soldiers tied up Shadrach, Meshach, and Abednego. When they threw them into the fire, the flames jumped out and burned up the soldiers. Shadrach, Meshach, and Abednego fell into the roaring flames. Suddenly the king leaped to his feet. He couldn't believe his eyes! He questioned the men near him. *(Man #1 and Man #2 up)*

King Nebuchadnezzar: Didn't we tie up three men? And didn't we throw them into the fire? But look! I can see four men. They aren't tied up. They are *walking* around in the fire. The fourth man looks like a god! *(Man #1 and Man #2 down)*

Narrator: The king ran to the blazing furnace. He stood as close as he dared and called out to the men inside.

King Nebuchadnezzar: Shadrach, Meshach, Abednego. You servants of the most high God, come out here!

Narrator: The three Israelites stepped out of the fire. Suddenly the fourth man was gone!

King Nebuchadnezzar: I don't understand it. Your clothes aren't burned. Your hair isn't burned. You don't even smell of smoke! I praise your God. He must have sent his angel to save you from the fire.

Shadrach: We trusted the Lord to save us.

Meshach: We were willing to die rather than serve any god but the Lord.

Abednego: The Lord was with us in the blazing furnace.

King Nebuchadnezzar: I am making a new law. Anyone who says anything bad about Shadrach, Meshach, and Abednego's God will be killed and his house torn down. No other god can save His people like this.

Narrator: Then the king promoted Shadrach, Meshach, and Abednego and gave them a more important place in his government. The Lord saved Shadrach, Meshach, and Abednego because they loved and worshiped Him. And we, too, can trust the Lord to walk with us in all our troubles.

Three Brave Men

(tune: "Three Blind Mice")

Three brave men; three brave men
Wouldn't worship the idol; wouldn't worship the idol.
The king put them in a furnace hot,
But the Lord's power he had forgot.
God kept them safe; burned up they were not.
These three brave men; three brave men.
Four men in the fire, four men in the fire
Who was the fourth? Who was the fourth?
He was the Lord of the earth and sky.
He always listens to us when we cry.

The Fourth Man

Three men who would not bow down
    (Hold up three fingers.)
Though the idol wore a crown.
    (Shake head.)
Four men walking in the flame.
    (Hold up four fingers.)
One was God the Lord by name.
    (Hold up one finger; point upward.)
He had answered the men's prayers.
    (Fold hands; bow head.)
He loves me and always cares.
    (Point to self.)

At the Tip of Their Tongues

Daniel 6:1-28

(Daniel, enemy, King Darius, 4 lions)

Daniel *(pointer)*
1   1 1/2" brown pom
2   5 MM eyes
face #2 and chin
flesh, red felt
braid; sequin
small amount polyester stuffing
2" velcro
Glue sleeve trim to *back* side of sleeves and hands #1 to *front* side of sleeves, robe #2, so when they are glued together they are in the correct places. Gather hat crown #1 where shown. Stuff lightly with polyester to round out as if head is inside. Glue to top of pom. Fasten hat band #1 around head being sure to fasten to hat crown and pom.

King Darius *(thumb)*
1   1 1/2" gray pom
2   5 MM eyes
face #3
flesh, white, purple felt

1 jewelry 3-ring crown
1 jewelry bell cap
braid; sequin
1 1/2" velcro
Do not glue velcro to body first! Glue robe to body. Trim cloak #1 with braid. Fasten robed body inside cloak, turning cloak down over robe as indicated. Attach velcro to back of cloak. Add sequin to robe. Glue bell cap into 3-ring crown. Glue this entire crown to head.

Enemy *(pinky)*
1   1 1/2" black pom
2   5 MM eyes
face #4
flesh, green, yellow felt
trim; sequin
black embroidery floss
1 3/4" velcro
Glue coat #1 to robe where indicated. Add trim. Dip floss in white glue and allow to dry. This will be used for eyebrows and mustache. Add eyebrows and mustache to face where shown by x's. Fasten headband around head. Cover ends with sequin trim.

Lions *(middle and ring)*
4   1 1/2" gold poms
12 1/4" white poms
8   5 MM eyes
gold, white, black felt
4   1" pieces velcro
Glue white poms where indicated. Larger gold nose piece is attached at forehead and over 2 cheek poms. Black triangle is joined to this and extends to chin pom. Glue each ear piece together at bottom edge before attaching to head at corners of face.

Sign *(hand)*
green, tan, brown felt

1 1/2" *hook* velcro

2" velcro

Glue sign front to back where indicated. Fasten sign to post where shown. Fringe grass #6 and add to bottom of post. Attach 2" velcro to back side of rocks. Secure the *hook* velcro to the back of sign crosspiece. This hook side will adhere to the glove material to help hold sign in place. Add details to sign, bird, and rocks with marker.

Puppet Play

Narrator: The Israelites had been taken to the land of Babylon by their enemies. One of the Israelites named Daniel was only a young boy when he was captured. He was trained by the king to serve in the government of this strange land. Daniel grew up to be an important man to the king. *(Daniel up)* Although the Babylonians worshiped other gods, Daniel continued to worship the Lord. He loved God. Every day he talked to God in prayer.

Daniel: Dear Lord, thank You for taking care of me here in a land where there are so many false gods. Help me to tell the people about You. *(Daniel down)*

Narrator: Some of the Babylonians didn't like Daniel. They were very jealous of him because the king had given him such a special job in the government.

Enemy: *(Enemy up)* Daniel, Daniel, Daniel. I'm so tired of hearing about him all the time. Now the king wants to make him the most important man in the country. But my friends and I have a plan to fool the king and get rid of Daniel.

Narrator: Daniel's enemy went to the king with this evil plan.

King: *(King up)* What is this new rule you want me to make?

Enemy: You are the greatest king to ever live, so my friends and I want you to make a law that the people can't pray to any god but you for the next thirty days. Anyone who prays to any other god will be thrown into the lions' den.

King: Hmm. Do you *really* think I am the greatest king who ever lived? Very well, I will write this rule down so that it cannot be changed. *(King down)*

Narrator: Now this was exactly what Daniel's enemy wanted. He watched Daniel's house carefully. There he saw Daniel praying and thanking God just as he had always done. The enemy hurried back to the palace to tell the king. *(King up)*

Enemy: Didn't you write a law that no one could pray to anyone except you for thirty days? And doesn't it say that if anyone breaks that law he must be thrown into the lions' den?

Enemy: Daniel has broken that law. I just heard and saw him praying to his God. He must be thrown into the lions' den! *(Enemy down)*

Narrator: Daniel and the king were good friends. The king realized he had been tricked and was very unhappy about it. He tried to think of some way to save Daniel, *(Daniel up)* but at last he was forced to order him to be thrown down into the lions' den. *(Add sign)*

King: Put that heavy stone over the top of the den and I will seal it shut with my ring. Daniel, I hope your God will save you. *(King down; Lions up)*

Narrator: It was dark and cold inside the den. Daniel could feel the hot breath of the hungry lions as they came closer and closer to him. He prayed to the Lord and asked for His help.

Daniel: Lord, I ask You to help me. Please save me from these lions. Help the king to know that You are the only true God.

Narrator: Suddenly a bright light shone in the darkness. There stood an angel between Daniel and the hungry lions. Now, instead of pouncing upon Daniel and eating him, the lions were lying quietly in a corner of the den. He could see their bright yellow eyes and hear their heavy breathing.

Daniel: Thank You, God, for sending this angel and saving my life. I can sleep peacefully tonight because You are watching over me.

Narrator: The king didn't eat any supper that evening. He couldn't sleep at all. Very early the next morning he rushed out to the lions' den. *(King up)*

King: Daniel, Daniel. Are you all right? Was your God able to save you from the lions?

Daniel: Yes, my king. My God sent an angel to shut the lions' mouths. He has protected me because He knows I love Him and I have not done anything wrong.

King: That is wonderful! Lift Daniel out of the lions' den. *(Lions down; Remove sign)* I will write a new law that everyone in my kingdom must worship the God of Daniel because He is the living God. He saved Daniel from the power of the lions. There is no other God but Daniel's God!

Narrator: Because Daniel faithfully worshiped Him, the Lord answered Daniel's prayers. He saved Daniel's life and used him to tell others about the living God. The Lord loves to answer our prayers when we truly trust Him to help us. And like Daniel, we can remain faithful to the Lord, even when we are surrounded by people who do not know Him.

Daniel Was in the Lions' Den

(tune: "London Bridge")

Daniel was in the lions' den, lions' den, lions' den,
Daniel was in the lions' den because he prayed to God.

God's angel shut the lions' mouths, lions' mouths, lions' mouths,
God's angel shut the lions' mouths and protected Daniel.

The king was happy that Daniel was safe, Daniel was safe, Daniel was safe.
The king was happy that Daniel was safe and he worshiped God.

Faithful Daniel

Faithful Daniel loved the Lord
  (Point upward.)
And knelt each day to pray.
  (Fold hands, bow head.)
But his enemies told the king,
  (Cup hands around mouth.)
Who sent poor Daniel away.
  (Point away from self.)
Into the hungry lions' den
  (Rub stomach, lick lips.)
He put him with great sorrow.
  (Hang head; look sad.)
The king said, "You will have to stay
  (Shake index finger.)
All night—'til sunrise tomorrow."
  (Make arch over head with arms.)
God sent an angel to the den
  (Point downward.)
And saved this faithful man.
The king and all the people there
  (Extend arms at sides.)
Praised God throughout the land.
  (Clap hands.)

A Marriage Made in Heaven

Esther 1:1—9:5

(Esther, Mordecai, King Xerxes, Haman, Queen Vashti)

Esther *(pointer)*
1 1 1/2" brown pom
2 5 MM eyes
face #7
flesh, orange, white felt; striped material
metallic braid, 3 sequins
2" velcro
Glue yoke #1 to robe. Attach coat #1 and trim it. Make headband of braid. Use sequin for pin at throat. Earrings are sequins glued beside face. Blush the cheeks. Use removable crown from "If I Were King" at proper place in story.

Mordecai *(thumb)*
1 1 1/2" gray pom
2 5 MM eyes
face #13
flesh, blue felt; striped material
1 1/2" velcro
Cut striped material crosswise and use for belt and headband.

King Xerxes *(Middle)*
1 1 1/2" black pom
2 5 MM eyes
face #2
flesh, white, purple felt
gold trim; gold metallic chenille stick; gold filigree or sequin
jewelry bell cap and 3-ring crown
2" velcro
Do not glue velcro to body first! Glue robe to body. Trim cloak #1 with braid. Fasten robed body inside cloak, turning cloak down over robe as indicated. Attach velcro to back of cloak. Add narrow braid and filigree to robe. Bend one end of chenille over several times to form a broad top. Fasten other end of chenille to robe. Glue hands #1 over chenille as if king is holding scepter. Attach bell cap to 3-ring crown and secure entire crown to head.

Haman *(pinky)*
1 1 1/2" brown pom
2 5 MM eyes
face #4
tan, lavender, yellow-green felt
polyester stuffing
black floss
gold trim
2" velcro
Attach coat #2 over robe and trim coat at neck and bottom. Dip floss in white glue and allow to dry. This will be used for eyebrows and mustache. Add eyebrows and mustache to face where shown by x's. Gather hat crown #1 where shown. Stuff lightly with polyester to round out as if head is inside. Glue to top of pom. Fasten hat band #1 around head being sure to fasten to hat crown and pom.

Vashti *(ring)*
1 1 1/2" gold pom

2 5 MM eyes
face #5
flesh, teal felt; striped material
gold loop trim
1 3/4" velcro

Fasten drape #1 over robe. Use marker to add fold lines to drape. Trim both edges of drape. Use trim for headband. Cut 2 tiny pieces of loop trim and glue to each side of face for earrings. Blush the cheeks.

Palace *(hand)*

tan felt

Cut two pieces of palace pattern. Add details to front with marker and glue to back piece.

Puppet Play

Narrator: Among the Jews who were captured and carried off to Persia was a beautiful young girl named Esther. *(Esther up)* She had no family to care for her, so she lived with an older cousin named Mordecai. *(Mordecai up)* Mordecai was a gatekeeper for the king. He loved Esther like his own daughter and taught her to always serve the Lord. And Esther was ready when the Lord had a special plan for her in this strange land. *(Esther and Mordecai down)* It all began when King Xerxes gave a great party for all his friends. *(King Xerxes up)*

King Xerxes: Bring me Queen Vashti. Be sure she wears the royal crown.

Narrator: But the queen refused to obey. *(Vashti up)*

Queen Vashti: I won't come!

King Xerxes: Then you are no longer my queen! I will have a beauty contest and pick the girl that pleases me most to be my new wife. *(Vashti down)*

Narrator: The king's servants brought all the beautiful girls in the land to the palace. *(Add palace)* Esther was among them.

(Esther up) And wonder of wonders, the king chose her to be the new queen! *(Mordecai up)* One day Mordecai sent a message to Esther that saved the king from some men who planned to kill him. *(Esther and Xerxes down; Haman up)* There was an important man named Haman in the king's court. He was the king's best friend and everyone bowed to him when he passed by. Everyone? Well, everyone except Mordecai who was a Jew and bowed only to the Lord. When Haman saw that Mordecai never honored him, he was furious. *(Mordecai down)*

Haman: What do you mean, Jews bow only to their god? I'm as important as their god! If they won't bow to me, then I'll destroy all of them!

Narrator: Haman went to the king and convinced him that the Jews were troublemakers and should all be destroyed. *(Haman down)*

Mordecai: *(Mordecai up)* Tell Esther to go to the king and beg for mercy for our people.

Esther: *(Esther up)* Tell Mordecai I can't do that! No one can enter the inner courtyard unless the king has sent for him. If he does he will be killed. The only change to that rule is if the king holds out his gold scepter to that person. Then he can live.

Narrator: Nobody but Mordecai knew that Esther was a Jewess. And he believed that God would use her to save them.

Mordecai: The Lord has chosen you as queen for a reason. Now is your chance to save your people! *(Mordecai down)*

Narrator: Esther was afraid of Haman and afraid of the king. But she loved Mordecai and remembered all the stories he had told her of the Lord's power. She would trust the Lord. For three days and nights Esther and all the Jews went without eating or drinking. Instead, they prayed to the Lord. Then Esther went to the king. Her knees were shaking. *(King Xerxes up)* And the king—held—out—his—scepter! Esther's hands trembled so that she could scarcely touch it.

King Xerxes: What do you want, Queen Esther? I will give you even half of my kingdom if you want it.

Esther: I—I would like you and Haman to come to dinner tonight. *(Esther down)*

Narrator: That night was the first of two dinners that the king and Haman ate with Esther. The night between the two meals, the king couldn't sleep. He commanded a servant to read the book of records to him. And there he found that nothing had been done to honor Mordecai for saving his life. Well, he would have to do something about that! Haman couldn't sleep that night either. He decided to build a tall gallows and hang Mordecai on it. Early the next morning he went to ask permission to hang Mordecai. *(Haman up)*

King Xerxes: What should I do to honor someone very greatly?

Narrator: Haman was sure the king meant him, so he told the king how he would like to be honored.

Haman: He should wear one of the king's own robes and ride one of the royal horses with a royal symbol on its head. Then an important man should lead him through the streets and announce, "This is what is done for the man the king wants to honor!"

King Xerxes: Go quickly, Haman. Do all this for Mordecai the Jew.

Narrator: What? Honor the man he wanted to hang? It was a horrible day for Haman. When he came to dinner that night, he was very upset. *(Esther up)*

King Xerxes: What do you want, Queen Esther?

Esther: Please save my life and the lives of all my people, the Jews, here in Persia.

King Xerxes: I did not know you were a Jew. Who would dare to do such a thing to you and your family?

Esther: This enemy here at the table—Haman.

Narrator: The king was furious. Haman trembled in terror. One of the king's servants told him about the gallows Haman had built for Mordecai.

King Xerxes: Hang Haman on it! *(Haman and King Xerxes down)*

Narrator: The king wrote another law allowing the Jews to defend themselves and promised to protect them. Yes, the Lord had a special plan for Esther. And He has a special plan for your life as well.

Queen Esther

(tune: "London Bridge")

Esther was a lovely queen,
   Lovely queen, lovely queen.
Esther was a Jewish queen
   In the land of Persia.

Esther saved God's people there,
   People there, people there.
Esther saved the Israelites
   Because she trusted God.

Trusting Esther

Esther prayed to God above;
   (Fold hands; bow head.)
Trusted His Word and felt His love.
   (Cross arms over heart.)
God did answer Esther's prayer
   (Nod head.)
And showed to her His love and care.
   (Cross arms over heart.)
I can trust the Lord today
   (Point to self.)
Wherever I am, at home or at play.
   (Extend hands to sides, palms up.)

God's Little Lamb

Luke 2:1-20

(Mary, Joseph, Baby Jesus, Shepherd #1, Shepherd #2, Angel)

Mary *(pointer)*
1 1/2" brown pom
2 5 MM eyes
face #7
Flesh, light blue, white felt
2" velcro
Add belt #1 to robe. Fold and glue headscarf #2 around face. Blush the cheeks.

Joseph *(middle)*
1 1 1/2" black pom
2 5 MM eyes
face #2
flesh, gold, maroon, brown felt
2" velcro
Glue belt #1 to robe. Fasten coat #1 to robe where indicated.

Manger *(thumb)*
gray, light yellow felt
Attach hay to manger where indicated.

Baby Jesus *(thumb)*
1 1/2" brown pom
face #1
flesh, white felt
Attach baby blanket #3 to manger where indicated. Glue head pom over blanket and hay at x. Add eyes and swaddling cloth marks with marker.

Shepherd #1 *(ring)*
1 1 1/2" black pom
2 5 MM eyes
face #3
tan, green felt; striped material
1 brown chenille stem
2" velcro
Cut striped material crosswise for belt and headband. Glue belt #1 to robe. Attach coat #1 to robe. Fasten headband around pom. Join sheep to lower corner of robe as shown. Cut a 3" length of chenille and shape into a crook. Attach to robe and add hand #1 as shown.

Sheep (Shepherd #1)
1 1" white pom
1 1/4" black pom
2 4 MM eyes
black felt
Glue black pom for nose. Attach ears #8. Join sheep to lower corner of shepherd's robe.

Shepherd #2 *(pinky)*
1 1/2" gray pom
2 5 MM eyes
face #15
tan, brown, yellow felt; striped material
1 brown chenille stem
1 3/4" velcro
Glue belt #1 to robe. Fasten headband around pom. Cut a 3" length of chenille and

shape into a crook. Attach to robe and add hand #1 as shown.

Angel *(pinky and middle)*
Use from story, "The Last Laugh." This angel will be moved around as needed for story.

Stable *(hand)*
brown, tan felt
2" velcro
Add roof to stable where indicated. Glue front to back piece.
Add details to front with marker.

Puppet Play

Narrator: When Adam and Eve sinned in the Garden of Eden, God promised to send a Savior to take the punishment for their sin. Hundreds and hundreds of years passed. Now, at long last, God was going to keep His promise. He sent an angel to a young girl named Mary. *(Angel and Mary up)* When Mary saw the angel she was frightened. She had never seen an angel before.

Angel: Don't be afraid, Mary. God knows that you love Him very much. You are going to be the mother of a baby boy. The baby will be very special. He will not have a human father, but will be God's own Son. His name will be Jesus. God can do everything!

Mary: I will serve the Lord. Let all this happen as you promise.

Narrator: Suddenly the angel was gone. *(Angel down)* Mary was going to be the wife of a kind man named Joseph. *(Joseph up)* Joseph saw an angel one night while he was sleeping and the angel told him the same thing he had told Mary. How happy Mary and Joseph were as they talked about and planned for the wonderful baby God was sending to them! They prepared a special place in their little home in Nazareth that would be just for Jesus. Then something happened to change their plans. All the peo-

ple in the land were ruled by the Romans. They had to obey whatever the Romans told them. Now the Roman king ordered all the people to go to their own towns to have their names written down on a list. Joseph's hometown was far to the south in the city of Bethlehem. So Mary and Joseph prepared to make the long trip. Mary carefully packed the soft strips of cloth she had made for the baby. Then down through the countryside they went, slowly moving along. At last they came to Bethlehem. Now everything would be all right. They would find a warm, dry place to sleep. But every inn was already full of people. There were even people sleeping in the streets.

Joseph: I'm so sorry, Mary. I have gone all over Bethlehem, knocking on doors and asking for a room. There just isn't any place left for us to stay tonight except with the animals in a stable.

Mary: That will be all right, Joseph. It will be quiet there and we will be warm and dry. *(Add stable)*

Narrator: Soon Mary and Joseph were settled in the small stable. Camels and donkeys were standing and lying all around them. They were sheltered there. Now no rude soldiers could shout at them or misuse the Lord's name. No crowd stared at them. It was a special, private place where God could give them His Son. There Mary's baby was born. She wrapped Him gently in the soft cloths she had brought. Joseph filled a stone feeding box with fresh clean hay and laid a blanket over it. Mary lovingly laid the baby in the manger. *(Baby Jesus up)*

Mary: Thank you, Joseph. Jesus will sleep well here. He is out of the cold wind and no animal can harm him. *(Mary, Joseph and Jesus down; remove Joseph)*

Narrator: Yes, God had kept His promise. His own Son, Jesus, was born. Mary and Joseph were happy and thanked the Lord. But they weren't the only ones who were glad that night. All the angels in heaven were delighted because Jesus was born. And they hurried to tell others about Him. Near Bethlehem, some shepherds were taking care of their sheep in the fields. *(Shepherd #1 up; add Shepherd #2 to pinky)* They were quietly talking together and nodding sleepily when suddenly there stood an angel, right in front of them! *(Move Angel to middle finger; Angel up)* And a bright, bright light shone all around them. The shepherds trembled in fear.

Angel: Don't be afraid. I bring you good news! Everybody will be happy when they hear it. Today your Savior was born in Bethlehem. He is wrapped up and lying in an animal's feeding box.

Narrator: Instantly the whole sky was filled with angels, all praising God. They said, "Give glory to God in Heaven, and let there be peace on earth to the people who please God." And then, as suddenly as they had come, the angels were gone! The bright light faded away and it was dark again. *(Angel down; Remove Angel)*

Shepherd #1: Let's go to Bethlehem and see the baby!

Shepherd #2: Let's see for ourselves what the Lord told us about!

Narrator: The shepherds hurried over the hills and fields to Bethlehem. They ran down the streets, through the crowds, zigzagged through donkeys and camels, and came at last to the stable. They stopped so fast, they ran into each other. Breathless, they peeked in. There was Joseph feeding a donkey. *(Replace Joseph on middle finger; Joseph up)* There was Mary bending over a feeding box. *(Mary up)* And there, cuddled up on the hay was baby Jesus! *(Jesus up)* He was sound asleep. First, the shepherds knelt down and thanked God for His Son. They told Mary and Joseph all about the angels and their message. Then the shepherds went back to their sheep in the fields. But that wasn't all—they told everyone they met that Jesus, their Savior, was born.

(Shepherds #1 and #2 down) Did you know that Jesus was born to be your Savior too? He was! Have you thanked God for Him? Have you told anyone about Him? He wasn't just any baby—He is God's Son!

The Shepherds

(tune: "Praise Him, Praise Him")

Shepherds watched their sheep out in the field by night,
Long ago, long ago.
When the sky was filled with song and angels bright.
From heaven's glow, heaven's glow.

"In the town of Bethlehem this very night
Christ is born, Christ is born."
Sang the angels from the heavens filled with light,
"Christ is born, Christ is born."

"Let us go to Bethlehem and see this sight.
We'll leave our sheep, leave our sheep,"
Said the shepherds, who were filled with great delight.
"We cannot sleep, cannot sleep."

Baby Jesus

Mary laid Jesus
    (Hold up finger.)
In a manger bed
    (Lay finger in palm of other hand.)
Right beside the animals;
    (Extend hands to sides, palms up.)
In the stable shed.
    (Touch fingertips of both hands together to indicate roof.)
Shepherds came to see Him;
    (Place hand above eyes.)
Sent by God above.
    (Point upward.)
They told many others
    (Hold up all fingers.)
About God's gift of love.
    (Cross hands over heart.)

A Blessing in Disguise

Matthew 2:1-23

(Mary, Child Jesus, Wise Men #1, #2, #3, King Herod)

Wise Man #1 (pointer)

1 1 1/2" black pom
2 5 MM eyes
face #16
brown, red, gray felt
gold trim, jewelry filigree
2" velcro
Glue sleeve trim to *back* side of sleeves robe #2 and hands #1 to *front* side of sleeves so when they are glued together they are in the correct places. Trim bottom of robe. Glue hands to hold gift #1 so gift is loose from robe. Cut two #1 hatband pieces and wind these around face and head to form turban. Decorate front of turban with filigree.

Wise Man #2 (middle)

1 1 1/2" black pom
2 5 MM eyes
face #13
tan, dark green, lavender, gold felt
gold trim

1 3/4" velcro
Trim bottom of robe. Glue drape #2 to front of robe and cloak #2 to back of robe. Add details with marker. Fasten hands #1 to inside of sleeves #2. Glue hands to gift #2. Attach sleeves to shoulders of robe. Gift will be left free of body. Gather hat crown #1 where shown. Stuff lightly with polyester to round out as if head is inside. Glue to top of pom. Attach headdress side piece to each side of face and at top to hat crown. Fasten headband around head being sure to fasten to hat crown and side pieces.

Wise Man #3 (ring)

1 1 1/2" gray pom
2 5 MM eyes
face #3
flesh, purple, bright blue, brown felt
gold trim
2" velcro
Do not glue velcro to body first! Glue robe to body and trim bottom of robe. Trim cloak #1 with braid. Fasten robed body inside cloak, turning cloak down over robe as indicated. Attach velcro to back of cloak. Glue hands to each side of gift #3. Join hands to front edges of robe but leave gift loose from robe.

King Herod (thumb)

1 1 1/2" white pom
2 5 MM eyes
Face #15
flesh, cerise, dark teal, yellow felt
metallic trim; 1/2" bright colored pom or bead
jewelry bell cap; sequin
Trim robe. Glue belt of trim to robe. Trim front of robe with sequin. Attach coat #2 to robe and trim as shown. Fasten bell cap to top of head for crown. Glue pom or bead in bell cap to complete crown.

Mary (*pinky*)
Use from story "God's Little Lamb."

Child Jesus (*pointer*)
1   3/4" or 1/2" brown pom
face #1, baby body
flesh, light blue felt
1/8" blue ribbon
1 1/2" *hook* side velcro
Attach ribbon belt to baby robe. Add eyes with marker. The hook velcro will attach to Mary and child can be added at proper place in story.

House (*hand*)
tan felt
2" velcro
Cut 2 pieces of house pattern. Add details to front with marker. Glue to back piece.

Star (*hand*)
gold felt
gold glitter
3/4" *hook* velcro
Cut 2 pieces of star pattern. Glue front to back piece. Add black background with marker, leaving star and rays. Cover star and ray area with thin coat white glue. Sprinkle on glitter and allow to dry. Shake off excess glitter. After first use, star can be reattached to hand with velcro above house at proper place in story.

Puppet Play

Narrator: After Jesus was born, Mary and Joseph moved into a small house in Bethlehem. Mary (*Mary up*) lovingly took care of God's little Son. (*Add Child Jesus to Mary*) While Jesus was growing, God was busy telling some men about His Son. (*Mary and Jesus down; Wise men #1, #2, #3 up*) These men studied the stars and were called wise men. One night as they sat looking at the sky, they gasped in wonder. (*Add star*)

Wise Man #3: Look up there! There is a bright, bright star I have never seen before!

How could I have missed it all these years?

Wise Man #2: You did not miss it, my friend. I am quite sure it was never there before this night.

Wise Man #1: What can it mean? We must learn more about it.

Narrator: The wise men studied until at last they felt they understood the reason for the shining new star.

Wise Man #1: It is a sign that there is a new king born to the Jews.

Wise Man #2: We must follow it and worship him.

Wise Man #3: Let us also take gifts to honor this king.

Narrator: The wise men packed their gifts and supplies, climbed on their camels, and started out towards the land of the Jews. They had the star to guide them. After many, many days they came to the king's palace in Jerusalem. (*Remove star*) King Herod was very surprised to see these important men. (*King Herod up*)

King Herod: What do you want? Why are you here?

Wise Man #1: Where is the baby who was born to be the king of the Jews?

Wise Man #2: We saw his star from our home in the east.

Wise Man #3: We have come to worship him.

Narrator: When Herod heard about a new Jewish king, he was very upset. He quickly sent for his advisors and asked them where this king was to be born. "God's Word says he will be born in Bethlehem." King Herod hastily thought of a plan. He secretly called the wise men to his throne room.

King Herod: When did you first see this star?

Wise Man #1: About two years ago, your majesty.

King Herod: Hmmm. Well, go to Bethlehem. The child you are looking for should be there. Look carefully for him. When you have found him and honored him, come tell me. Then I can go honor him too. *(King Herod down)*

Narrator: The wise men were puzzled. Had they made a mistake about the star? But as soon as the wise men climbed back on their camels, there was the star again. *(Add star)*

Wise Man #2: It is the same star we saw in the east! Praise the Lord!

Wise Man #3: See, it is moving just ahead of us, leading the way to Bethlehem.

Wise Man #1: Look—it has stopped over that house. *(Add house below star)* That must be where the king is.

Narrator: The camels knelt down and the wise men excitedly climbed off. They went into the house. There they saw Jesus and His mother, Mary. *(Mary and Jesus up)*

Wise Man #2: We saw your star in the east. I brought you sweet smelling frankincense.

Wise Man #3: We are here to worship you, little king. Here is a gift of gold for you.

Wise Man #1: You are the one God promised long ago. My gift is myrrh. *(Mary and Jesus down)*

Narrator: That night the wise men went to sleep with glad hearts. They planned to return to King Herod and tell him where to find Jesus. But God warned the wise men in a dream not to go back to Herod. They obeyed the Lord and returned home a different way. *(Wise Men #1, #2, #3 down)* As soon as they had left, God sent an angel to warn Joseph. "Get up and take Jesus and Mary to Egypt. Herod is going to start looking for the child to kill him. Stay in Egypt until I tell you to return." Joseph jumped up from his bed. Before the night was over, Joseph, Mary, and Jesus were on their way to Egypt. Herod was furious when he realized the wise men weren't coming back. *(King Herod up)*

King Herod: Send soldiers to Bethlehem immediately. Kill all the boys two years old or younger!

Narrator: But God protected His Son. Jesus, Mary, and Joseph stayed in Egypt until wicked King Herod died.

Three Wise Men

(tune: "Three Blind Mice")

Three wise men, three wise men;
See how they came, see how they came.
They all followed a big, bright star;
Trav'ling from countries so very far,
To worship the King of the Jews from afar.
Three wise men, three wise men.

The Journey of the Wise Men

Three men followed a big, bright star
   (Hold up three fingers.)
To find a wonderful king.
   (Hold hands in circle above head to indicate crown.)
Traveling far from their home country
Rich gifts to Him they'd bring.
   (Extend hands.)
At last they found the little king
And gave to Him each gift.
   (Extend hands.)
They went back to their homes again
Riding on camels swift.
   (Move fingers quickly in palm of other hand to indicate running.)

Rise and Shine

Mark 5:21-24, 35-43; Luke 8:40-56

(Jesus, Jairus, Mother, Little Girl, Man #1, Man #2)

Jesus (pointer)
1   1 1/2" brown pom
2   5 MM eyes
face #3 and chin
flesh, white, red felt
2" velcro
Leave small pom space between face and chin for mustache. Attach drape #1 to robe as shown.

Jairus (middle)
1   1 1/2" black pom
2   5 MM eyes
face #2
flesh, dark yellow, orange felt; striped material
2" velcro
Glue belt #1 to robe. Attach coat #1 where indicated. Gather hat crown #1 where shown. Stuff lightly with polyester to round out as if head is inside. Glue to top of pom. Fasten hat band #1 around head being sure to fasten to hat crown and pom.

Mother (ring)
1   1 1/2" black pom
2   5 MM eyes
face #11
flesh, pink felt; striped material
metallic trim
2" velcro
Add trim and belt to robe. Cut 2 tiny pieces of loop trim and glue to each side for earrings. Fold and glue headscarf #2 around face. Blush the cheeks.

Little Girl (thumb)
2   1" black poms
2   4 MM eyes
face #12
flesh, light blue felt; striped material
1 3/4" velcro
Two figures are made for the little girl. One is for her "sleeping" and the other after Jesus has raised her. Make the eyes for the sleeping child with permanent ink fine-tip felt pen. Fold scarves #1 around each head. Blush the cheeks only on the open-eyed girl.

Man #1 (pinky)
1   1 1/2" gray pom
2   5 MM eyes
face #13
flesh, gray, lavender felt
sequin
1" velcro
Add sequin trim to side of head band.

Man #2 (pinky)
1   1 1/2" gold pom
2   5 MM eyes
face #16
flesh, lavender felt
1" velcro
Fasten headband around head.

House *(hand)*
Use from story "A Blessing in Disguise."

Puppet Play

Narrator: Jesus was a busy man. *(Jesus up)* Crowds of people waited for Him everywhere He went. Some of them wanted to hear Jesus tell stories about His heavenly Father. Some wanted to see Him do some great miracle. And some wanted Jesus to make them well again. Yes, everywhere Jesus went there were people pushing and shoving just to get near Him. Jairus *(Jairus up)* hurried through the streets of Capernaum and out to the lake. He could see a great crowd of people just ahead of him. Jesus was somewhere in that crowd. But where?

Jairus: Excuse me. May I get through, please? Oops! Sorry. I didn't mean to step on your foot. Pardon me, please.

Narrator: Jairus pushed and twisted his way through all the people. He just *had* to reach Jesus in time! Everything depended on it. Jairus squeezed through a tiny opening between a soldier and an old man. He ran to Jesus and bowed down.

Jairus: Jesus! My little girl is very, very sick. Oh please come and touch her. I know You can make her well again.

Jesus: Yes, of course I will come.

Narrator: Some people moved aside to let them through. Jairus led the way. But as he looked back he could see the crowd closing in around Jesus. He pushed his way back to Jesus' side again.

Jairus: Hurry, Jesus! Did I tell you she was my only daughter?

Jesus: I am coming, Friend.

Narrator: Jairus was getting worried. People swarmed around Jesus like bees around flowers. They were talking to Him—touching Him—stopping Him. Jesus would never get there in time this way! Jairus remembered how white his little girl's face had been when he left her. She hadn't even opened her eyes when he kissed her and said good-bye. Now Jairus was desperate.

Jairus: Lord, please hurry! She is dying!

Jesus: Yes, Friend. I am coming as quickly as I can.

Narrator: Suddenly Jairus spotted two familiar faces in the crowd. They were some of his servants. *(Men #1 and #2 up)* The men pushed through the mob and stopped in front of Jairus.

Man #1: I am sorry, Master.

Jairus: You mean ... ?

Man #2: Your daughter is dead, Sir. There is no need to bother the teacher now.

Narrator: Jairus hung his head. Tears filled his eyes. They ran down his nose and cheeks. Too late! Oh, if only Jesus could have gotten there in time!

Jesus: Jairus.

Jairus: Yes, Lord?

Jesus: Don't be afraid. Believe in me. Your little girl will be well.

Narrator: Jairus wiped his face with his sleeve. The people didn't matter anymore. The only one who mattered was Jesus. Jesus led the way now. The crowd parted silently to let them through. Soon they came to Jairus' house. *(Add house)* There was much confusion. People stood around crying loudly. Jairus' wife *(Wife up)* was sobbing on the shoulder of a friend.

Jesus: Why are you all crying? The little girl isn't dead. She is just asleep.

Man #1: You are wrong. She is dead.

Man #2: Don't mislead our master. She died before we could reach You, Jesus.

Jesus: All of you must leave. Only her mother and father may stay. *(Men #1 and #2 down)*

Narrator: Then Jesus took three of His followers, the girl's mother, and Jairus with Him into the child's room. The little girl looked like she was asleep. *(Sleeping girl up)* Her mother began to cry. Jairus put his arm around his wife. He tried to swallow the lump in his throat. Hopefully, he turned to Jesus. Jesus bent over the child. He gently took her still, white hand in His strong, tanned one.

Jesus: My child, stand up!

Narrator: Jairus couldn't believe his eyes! The little girl's eyelids fluttered, then slowly opened. She yawned, sat up, and rubbed her eyes. *(Remove sleeping girl and replace with open-eyed girl)*

Little Girl: Oh, I feel so much better! I had such a good rest.

Narrator: Jairus helped his daughter up. To his delight, she began to walk around the room. Suddenly she stopped.

Little Girl: Why are all of you looking at me so strangely?

Narrator: The child ran to her mother and threw her arms around her.

Little Girl: I'm really hungry, Mother. May I have something to eat?

Narrator: Jesus laughed. It was a joyous laugh that filled the room to overflowing. The anxious crowd heard it and marveled.

Jairus laughed too. Jesus had answered his prayer.

The Little Girl

(tune: "Are You Sleeping?")

Jairus' daughter, Jairus' daughter,
Was very sick, and dying.
Then they sent for Jesus. Jairus went for Jesus.
He could help. He would help.

"Little girl, little girl,
Rise and stand. Stand right up."
The little girl got up. She stood right up,
And walked around; around the room.

Jesus and the Sick Girl

Jairus had a daughter
   (Hold up one finger.)
Who was very ill.
   (Look sad.)
The doctors couldn't help her
With medicine or pills.
   (Shake head.)
Jairus went to Jesus.
   (Move fingers quickly in palm of other hand to indicate running.)
"Help me, please," he said.
   (Extend hands.)
"If you don't, my daughter
I fear will soon be dead."
   (Hang head; look sad.)
Jesus went with Jairus
   (Move fingers in palm of other hand to indicate walking.)
And told her to arise.
   (Raise arms.)
From death to life He raised her
Right before their eyes.
   (Point to eyes.)

The More the Merrier

Matthew 14:31-21; Mark 6:32-44; Luke 9:10-17; John 6:1-14

(Jesus, Andrew, Boy, Man, Woman)

Jesus (*middle*)

Use from story "Rise and Shine."

Andrew (*pointer*)
1 1 1/2" red-brown pom
2 5 MM eyes
face #16
flesh, teal, dark teal felt; striped material
2" velcro
Glue belt #1 to robe. Attach coat #1 where indicated. Fasten headband around head.

Boy (*thumb*)
1 1" black pom
2 4 MM eyes
face #9, child body
flesh, yellow felt
metallic trim
1/8" yellow ribbon
miniature basket
1 1/2" velcro

Attach hand #2 to sleeves #1. Trim bottom of sleeves and robe. Glue sleeves to robe at shoulders. Use ribbon for headband. Fasten hands around basket handle, leaving basket free.

Man (*ring*)
1 1 1/2" black pom
2 5 MM eyes
face #3
flesh, red felt; striped material
polyester stuffing
2" velcro
Cut striped material crosswise for belt #1. Attach belt to robe. Gather hat crown #1 where shown and stuff lightly to round out. Glue down tightly so pom "hair" covers gathered edge.

Woman (*pinky*)
1 1 1/2" brown pom
2 5 MM eyes
face #11
flesh, lavender, light blue felt; striped material
1 3/4" velcro
Glue yoke #2 to robe. Add belt #1 to robe. This face has an extra cut for mouth. Glue face to head pom being sure to leave the top lip free to add facial expression. Attach one end of headscarf #2 to side of face. Wrap around head and secure scarf at other side of face and over shoulder. Blush the cheeks.

Hillside (*hand*)
dark green, green, light green, blue felt
small flowers
2" velcro
Glue hill #1 to back where indicated. Add hill #2 and hill #3 in same manner. Lake is attached last and over hill #3 where indicated. Fasten small flowers on hillside at x's.

Puppet Play

Narrator: Jesus *(Jesus up)* and His followers had been very busy. They had just come back from preaching and healing crowds of people. So many people kept coming and going around them that Jesus and His followers didn't even have time to eat. They were *so* tired.

Jesus: Come with me. We'll go to a quiet place where we can be alone and rest.

Narrator: They got in a boat and sailed peacefully across a beautiful, blue lake. Jesus' followers were beginning to relax. Soon they would be on the other shore where there would be no people. *(Add hillside)* But wait—what was that on the hillside? Oh no! The people had seen them leave and run around the lake ahead of them. Now another crowd was waiting for Jesus to come ashore! His followers were hoping that Jesus would send all the people away. But when Jesus saw the throng, He felt sorry for them.

Jesus: They are just like sheep without a shepherd to lead them. I will tell them more about my heavenly Father and His great love.

Narrator: Soon Jesus was sitting on the hillside with people all around Him. There were men who had walked for long distances. *(Man up)* Women had brought their wool and sat spinning as they listened. *(Woman up)* Some of them had brought their children to see Jesus. *(Man and Woman down)* And some children had come alone to hear Jesus tell stories. A little boy *(Boy up)* tried to see over the crowd. One of Jesus' followers *(Andrew up)* was sitting nearby. He noticed the boy's problem.

Andrew: Can you see Jesus, my child?

Boy: No, Sir. I'm just too little.

Andrew: My name is Andrew. I'll find a place for you. Just take hold of my hand and follow me. Well, now, what do you have in your basket?

Boy: My lunch. Mother thought I might get hungry so she packed a lunch for me.

Andrew: Mothers know that growing boys are always hungry, don't they? Make room for my young friend, please. There you are now. Right up front where you can see and hear everything.

Boy: Thank you, Sir.

Narrator: The little boy squeezed close to Jesus. He didn't want to miss a word. All that afternoon Jesus taught the people. The long shadowy fingers of evening were beginning to poke into the folds of the hills around the lake. But nobody left. Jesus' followers asked Him to send the people home so they could go buy food in the nearby towns and farms.

Jesus: You give them something to eat.

Narrator: Jesus' followers gasped. "Why even if we took all our money for a whole month, we wouldn't have enough money to buy that much bread!"

Jesus: How many loaves of bread do you have now? Go and see.

Narrator: The little boy was listening. It seemed that his friend could use his help. He tugged on the hem of Andrew's robe.

Boy: Sir, Jesus can have my lunch.

Andrew: That's very kind of you, Son. Come, let's go show it to Jesus. Here is a boy with five loaves of barley bread and two little fish, Master. But that isn't enough for this many people. There must be about 5,000 men here.

Narrator: Jesus looked right at the little boy. A smile spread across Jesus' face. He reached down and took the boy's basket.

Jesus: Tell the people to sit down. (*Man and Woman up*)

Narrator: Soon the people were sitting down in groups on the grassy hillside. Jesus reached into the basket and brought out the loaves of bread.

Jesus: Thank you, Father, for providing for all our needs. Bless this child for sharing what he has with us.

Narrator: Jesus broke the bread into pieces and began handing them to His followers. The little boy's eyes grew wide with astonishment. The more pieces Jesus broke off, the more pieces were left. Then He did the same thing with the fish. Soon everybody was eating bread and fish. The little boy was now sitting right beside Jesus. Every so often, he would look up into Jesus' face and Jesus would smile right back at him. It was a wonderful meal! When they had all finished eating, Jesus told His followers to pick up the uneaten food. (*Man and Woman down*)

Jesus: Don't waste anything.

Narrator: His followers gathered up all the food that was left. And it was enough to fill 12 large baskets! When he left the hillside for home that night, the little boy was full right up to his eyes. Oh yes, he was full of bread and fish, but better yet—his heart was full of the happiness that Jesus' love had put there. How glad he was that he had shared his small lunch with the Lord of all things! We can know that kind of happiness too. All we need to do is give Jesus what we have. It may seem small, but Jesus can make it more than enough for everyone in need.

The Little Boy's Lunch

(tune: "Jingle Bells")

Bread and fish, bread and fish
The little boy had brought
In his basket lunch that day
While the Master taught.

With Jesus Christ, Jesus Christ
The little boy did share.
The people ate 'till they were full
And there was food to spare.

A Boy Who Shared

Once a boy went to see
   (*Hand above eyes.*)
Jesus, who was at Galilee.
The boy overheard Jesus say,
   (*Cup hand around ear.*)
"Many people are here today.
   (*Hold up all fingers.*)
We need food for the people to eat.
   (*Point to mouth.*)
Where can we buy bread and meat?"
   (*Shake head.*)
Quickly the boy cried out loud,
   (*Cup hands around mouth.*)
"Here is my lunch to share with the crowd."
   (*Extend hands.*)
Jesus thanked God and the food was shared.
   (*Fold hands; bow head.*)
How happy He was for the boy who cared!
   (*Draw smile on face with finger; smile.*)
I can share too like that little boy,
   (*Point to self.*)
And that will fill Jesus' heart with joy.
   (*Point upward.*)

The Moment of Truth

Luke 15:11-32

(Father, Younger Son, Older Son, Gentile Man, 2 Pigs)

Younger Son (middle)

1   1 1/2" brown pom
2   5 MM eyes
face #6
flesh, yellow, green, dark yellow, moss green felt
1" *hook* velcro
2" velcro

Glue coat #2 to robe. A second costume is used for this puppet to show how he looked after wasting his inheritance. The robe and coat are a shade darker than the original ones and are cut into tatters. Dirt smudges are added with marker. Glue the *hook* velcro to this second costume so it can be added over the figure at the proper time in the story.

Father (pointer)

1   1 1/2" gray pom
2   5 MM eyes
face #2
flesh, blue, dark blue felt; striped material
2" velcro

Glue belt #1 to robe. Fasten coat #1 to robe where indicated. Gather hat crown #1 where shown. Stuff lightly with polyester to round out as if head is inside. Glue to top of pom. Fasten hatband #1 around head being sure to fasten to hat crown and pom.

Older Son (thumb)

1   1 1/2"gold pom
2   5 MM eyes
face #15
flesh, maroon felt; striped material
polyester stuffing
1 1/2" velcro

Attach drape #1 to robe. Gather hat crown #1 where shown and stuff lightly to round out. Glue down tightly so pom "hair" covers gathered edge.

Gentile Man (ring)

1   1 1/2" black pom
2   5 MM eyes
face #3
tan, orange, dark blue felt
2" velcro

Fasten belt #1 to robe. Fasten headband around head.

Pigs (pinky)

2   1 1/2" white poms
2   3/4" white poms
4   4 MM eyes
white, black, pink felt
2   1" velcro

Attach small pom to bottom of large pom. rim this smaller pom so it is a cone shape. Cut tip of cone square. Glue on pink nose. Add nostrils with marker. Lap ears #9 over and glue to top of head. Ears should droop over face and eyes should be high and close together. Cut one ear and several small irregular pieces of black felt for the spotted pig.

Sign *(hand)*
tan, brown, green felt
2" velcro
Cut 2 of sign #2. Glue these together. Fasten sign to post. Attach bush #1 to bottom of post. Add details to sign with marker. Depending on whether using right or left hand glove, draw "home" arrow pointing toward Father and "far country" toward pigs.

Puppet Play

Narrator: Jesus taught the people about His heavenly Father by telling them stories. The Jewish religious leaders complained because so many sinners were coming to listen to Jesus. So He told them this story about a man with two sons. *(Man, Younger Son, Older Son up)* The younger son was a self-centered, disobedient boy. One day he came to his father.

Younger Son: Give me my share of the property.

Father: Of course, Son. But what do you want it for now? I will take care of you so you won't need it until I die.

Younger Son: I'm not going to stay here and take orders from you. I want to enjoy my money and make my own decisions.

Narrator: The loving father divided the property between his two sons. The younger son then took all that was his and left home. *(Father and Older Son down)* He took a trip to a country that was far away. *(Add sign Far Country/Home)*

Younger Son: Now I can enjoy life. I don't have to obey anybody and I can make all my own decisions. I'm just going to enjoy life and party with my friends.

Narrator: At first things went fine. When people heard that the boy was rich, they were all eager to become his friends. But soon his money was all gone. He could no longer afford food for himself. He couldn't buy any more gifts for his friends. When they saw that his money was gone, his so-called friends all left him. You see, they didn't like him—they only liked what he could do for them.

Younger Son: Who needs them anyway? I can get a job to pay for my food and rent. I can sell some of my clothes too for extra money. I'll show them!

Narrator: But nobody wanted to hire him. *(Gentile Man up)*

Gentile Man: Hmmm. Have you had any job training?

Younger Son: No, Sir.

Gentile Man: Well then, the only job I can give you is feeding my pigs. *(Pigs up)*

Younger Son: But our God told us not to eat pork. My people never even raise pigs. That would be the worst job I could have!

Gentile Man: Sorry young fellow, but that's the best I can do. *(Gentile Man down)*

Narrator: So the boy took the job. It was hot, dirty, smelly work. His beautiful robe was soon torn and covered with mud. *(Add tattered robe)* Soon after he took the job, the land became very dry and there was no rain. There was not enough food to eat anywhere in the country.

Younger Son: I'm so hungry I would even eat the food these pigs eat! I've been very foolish. Why all of my father's servants have plenty of food. If I stay here, I'll die of hunger. There's just one thing to do—I'll return home. But what can I say to my father? *(Pigs down)*

Narrator: As he trudged toward home on

foot, he practiced what he would say to his father.

Younger Son: I'll say to him, "Father, I've sinned against God and done wrong to you. I'm not good enough to be your son, but I could be like one of your servants." Yes, that's what I'll say. Oh, I hope he will take me back!

Narrator: Long before the boy reached home, his father saw him coming. *(Father up)* He ran to meet him and hugged and kissed him. The son started to give his speech.

Younger Son: "Father, I've sinned against God and done wrong to you. I'm... "

Father: Hurry, my servants! Bring the new striped robe and put it on my son. Bring that beautiful gold ring I had made for him. Bring the hand-tooled leather sandals for his feet. Go get a fat calf and kill it for dinner. We're going to have a celebration!

Younger Son: Father, I'm not good enough to be your son, but I could be like one of your servants.

Father: Nonsense! You, my son, were dead, but now you are alive again! You were lost, but now you are found! Come, let's rejoice!

Narrator: When the older son heard what was going on in the house, he was so angry he wouldn't go in and join the party. His father came out to talk to him.

Father: Come on in, Son, and be glad with us.

Older Son: No! I served you like a slave for all these years and obeyed you in everything. But you never even killed a goat for me to have a party with my friends. My brother wasted all your money and broke your heart. Yet when he comes home, you give him a great big party!

Father: Dear son, don't you know that all I have is yours? But we have to celebrate and be happy. Your brother was dead, but now he is alive. He was lost, but now he is found.

Narrator: Then Jesus said, "In the same way there is joy before the angels of God when one sinner changes his heart." Yes, God loves us like the father in the story loved his younger son.

The Son Who Left Home

(tune: "Twinkle, Twinkle Little Star)

Once a father had a son
Who ran away to have some fun.
Far from home, disobedient and bad,
The young son felt alone and sad.
"I'll go home again," said he.
"And ask my father to forgive me."

The father was waiting for his boy.
To see him again would bring great joy.
When he came home, the father said,
"How good to see you, my son who was dead.
You were lost, but now you are found.
My love for you knows no bounds."

A Father's Love

A boy took his money and left his home.
    (Touch fingertips to indicate roof.)
Far from his father he began to roam.
    (Move fingers to indicate walking.)
Soon he spent his money and was all alone.
    (Hold up finger.)
He ate with the pigs and began to moan.
    (Look sad.)
"I'll ask my father to forgive me," he said.
"I'll ask God too," and tears he shed.
    (Point to eyes.)
The boy went back home to his father's love.
    (Cross hands over heart.)
Then the father and son thanked God above.
    (Fold hands; bow head.)
The heavenly Father will forgive me too
    (Point to self.)
When I pray to God and ask Him to.
    (Fold hands; bow head.)

A Matter of Life and Death

John 11:1-45

(Jesus, Martha, Mary, Lazarus, Man #1, Man #2)

Jesus (pointer)
Use from story "Rise and Shine."

Martha (middle)
1 1 1/2" black pom
2 5 MM eyes
face #5
flesh, dark teal, peach felt; striped material
2" velcro
Glue belt #1 and yoke #1 to robe. Attach one end of headscarf #2 to side of face. Wrap around head and secure scarf at other side of face and over shoulder. Blush the cheeks.

Mary (ring)
1 1 1/2" red-brown pom
2 5 MM eyes
face #7
flesh, green, light green felt; striped material 2" velcro
Fasten yoke #3 and belt #1 to robe. Fold and glue headscarf #2 around face. Blush the cheeks.

Lazarus (thumb)
1 1 1/2" black pom
2 5 MM eyes
face #3
flesh, white felt
1 1/2" velcro
Use marker to make details of robe look like burial wrapping. Use two hatbands #1 and wrap these around head leaving face uncovered.

Man #1 (pinky)
1 1 1/2" brown pom
2 5 MM eyes
face #13
flesh, yellow, blue felt
polyester stuffing
1" velcro
Gather hat crown #1 where shown. Stuff lightly with polyester to round out as if head is inside. Glue to top of pom. Fasten hatband #1 around head being sure to fasten to hat crown and pom.

Man #2 (pinky)
Use man #2 from story "Rise and Shine."

Tomb (hand)
gray, green felt
2" velcro
Cut 2 tombs. Use marker to add details on tomb front where indicated. Add grass clumps #'s 2 and 4 to each side of doorway. Attach to back piece. Cut two stones (front and back). Fasten velcro to back stone and glue front to this back piece. Add stone to tomb, covering doorway, at beginning of story. Remove at proper time in the story.

Puppet Play

Narrator: Whenever He went to Jerusalem to worship in the temple, Jesus visited His friends, Martha, Mary, and Lazarus. They lived in the nearby town of Bethany. He loved them very much. One day, Lazarus became very sick. His two sisters sent a message to Jesus. *(Martha, Mary up)*

Martha: Tell Jesus that our brother is sick.

Mary: Yes, He will come right away and heal Lazarus as he has so many other sick people.

Narrator: But two days passed and Jesus didn't come. Lazarus got so sick that he died. Martha and Mary were very sad.

Mary: Why doesn't Jesus come?

Martha: Yes, Jesus has brought other people back to life. Even now He could raise Lazarus from death to live again.

Narrator: But the time came to bury Lazarus and Jesus still had not come. *(Men #1 and #2 up)*

Man #1: We have wrapped Lazarus' body with cloth strips and spices.

Man #2: The tomb is all ready for the burial. It is a beautiful cave in the white limestone hills just outside town.

Man #1: If Jesus was coming, He would have been here by now.

Narrator: So the sad little procession made its way from Bethany to the tomb in the hills outside town. *(Add tomb)* There they laid Lazarus inside the cave and placed a big stone over the entrance to keep out wild animals. *(Add stone)* *(Martha, Mary, Men #1 and #2 down)* Jesus was staying near the Jordan River where John had first baptized people. Jesus spoke to His followers. *(Jesus up)*

Jesus: It's time to go to Bethany. Our friend Lazarus has fallen asleep. But I am going there to wake him.

Narrator: His followers didn't understand that Lazarus had died. They thought Jesus just meant he was asleep and getting better.

Jesus: Lazarus is dead, but it will be all right. Many will believe in me because of what is going to happen.

Narrator: By the time Jesus arrived in Bethany, Lazarus had not only died, but been in the tomb for four days. When Martha heard Jesus was coming, she ran out to meet Him. *(Martha up)*

Martha: Lord, if You had been here, my brother wouldn't have died. But even now I know You can raise Lazarus from death to live again.

Jesus: Lazarus will rise and live again.

Martha: Yes, I know he will live again when time ends and all the dead are raised to live again.

Jesus: I am the Lord of life and death. The people who believe in me will live again even if they die. They will live with God forever. Do you believe this about me, Martha?

Martha: Oh, yes! You are the Lord, God's chosen one to save people from their sins. You are the Son of God.

Narrator: Martha hurried home to tell Mary that Jesus wanted to see her. *(Mary up)* Mary leaped up and rushed out to meet Jesus. When her friends saw Mary leave, they thought she was going to Lazarus' tomb to cry. They followed her to cheer her up. *(Men #1 and #2 up)* Mary knelt down by Jesus.

Mary: Oh, Lord, if You had just been here, my brother wouldn't have died!

Narrator: Mary began to cry very hard. The

people with her cried too. When Jesus saw everyone crying He was very sad.

Jesus: Where did you bury Lazarus?

Martha: Come see, Lord.

Narrator: Jesus began to cry too.

Man #1: Just see how much Jesus loved Lazarus.

Man #2: But if Jesus could even make blind men see, why didn't He keep Lazarus from dying?

Narrator: They all stopped in front of the cave tomb where Lazarus was buried.

Jesus: Move the stone away from the door.

Martha: But Jesus, he died four days ago. There will be a terrible smell.

Jesus: Martha, didn't I tell you that if you believed in me you would see the wonderful things God can do?

Narrator: The men worked together. One, two, three, heave!! The huge stone rumbled over the ground and away from the door. (*Remove stone*) Jesus looked up into Heaven and began to pray out loud.

Jesus: Father, thank You for always hearing me. Now I want these people to believe that You really did send me. Lazarus, come out!!!

Narrator: Everyone held their breath. Then there was a rustle of cloth. Something moved inside the cave. A figure wrapped in white clothes sat up on the rock shelf inside the tomb and then ... out came Lazarus. (*Lazarus up*) His hands and feet were still wrapped with pieces of cloth. Another cloth was partly wrapped around his face. There were shouts of joy and Martha and Mary ran forward to hug their brother.

Jesus: Take the cloth off of Lazarus and let him go!

Narrator: Many people came to believe in Jesus because He brought Lazarus back to life again.

Jesus Raised Lazarus

(tune: "Jesus Loves Me")

Jesus came when Lazarus died;
Told them to open the tomb up wide.
Jesus called Lazarus to come out.
"He's alive again!" the people did shout.
Yes, Jesus raised him,
Yes, Jesus raised him,
Yes, Jesus raised him,
He raised Lazarus from the dead.

Jesus Helps His Friends

Mary and Martha sat and cried
    (*Fold up two fingers.*)
For Lazarus, their brother, got sick and died.
    (*Finger in palm of other hand; close hand around finger.*)
Jesus came to help these two friends.
    (*Hold up three fingers.*)
Like God above, His love never ends.
    (*Point upward.*)
Away to the tomb they walked very sad;
    (*Move fingers in palm of other hand to indicate walking.*)
Their eyes filled with tears, they all felt bad.
    (*Point to eyes.*)
Jesus told them to move the stone;
    (*Extend hands forward, palms outward to indicate moving stone.*)
Then He prayed to God and called out alone,
    (*Fold hands, bow head.*)
"Lazarus, come out." And to their surprise
    (*Beckon towards self.*)
Lazarus walked out right before their own eyes.
    (*Walk in place stiffly.*)

Children Should Be Seen and Not Heard

Matthew 19:13-15; Mark 10:13-16; Luke 18:15-17

(Jesus, Peter, Mother #1, Mother #2, Father)

Jesus *(pinky)*
Use from story "Rise and Shine."

Peter *(thumb)*
1 1 1/2" black pom
2 5 MM eyes
face #3
flesh, moss green, dark yellow felt; striped material 2" velcro
Glue belt #1 to robe. Attach coat #1 to robe. Gather hat crown #1 where shown. Stuff lightly with polyester to round out as if head is inside. Glue to top of pom. Fasten hatband #1 around head being sure to fasten to hat crown and pom.

Mother #1 *(pointer)*
1 1 1/2" black pom
2 5 MM eyes
face #7
flesh, light pink, maroon felt
1/8" pink ribbon

2" velcro
Glue belt #1 to robe. Attach ribbon headband around head pom. Blush the cheeks.

Child #1 *(mother #1)*
1 1/2" brown pom
face #8, baby body
flesh, light blue-green felt
1/8" pink ribbon
Glue ribbon belt to robe. Use marker for eyes. Blush the cheeks. Attach to one side of mother.

Mother #2 *(middle)*
1 1 1/2" brown pom
2 5 MM eyes
face #5
flesh, light blue felt; striped material
2" velcro
Glue belt #1 to robe. Attach one end of headscarf #2 to side of face. Wrap around head and secure scarf at other side of face and over shoulder. Blush the cheeks.

Baby *(mother #2)*
1 1/2" brown pom
face #1
flesh, white felt
Fold and glue baby blanket #1 into a wrapped baby shape. Attach pom. Add eyes to face with marker. Fasten to mother #2. Blush cheeks.

Father *(ring)*
1 1 1/2" red-brown pom
2 5 MM eyes
face #3
flesh, green felt; striped material
polyester stuffing
1 3/4" velcro
Attach #1 hands inside sleeves of robe #2. Add belt #1 to robe. Gather hat crown and

round out with stuffing. Pull gathers tight. Glue down tightly so pom "hair" covers gathered edge.

Child #2 (father)
1 3/4" black pom
face #8
flesh, green felt; striped material
Glue belt to robe. Use marker for eyes. Attach to side of father. Glue father's hands to child's shoulders.

Hillside (hand)
Use from story "The More the Merrier."

Puppet Play

Narrator: Jesus was a busy and important man. (*Jesus up*) Crowds of people followed Him everywhere He went. Often He and His followers couldn't even eat a meal without being interrupted. Jesus felt sorry for the crowds and always took time to help them. But His followers grew tired of the mobs of pushing, shoving, demanding people. They decided they would protect Jesus from the multitudes who surrounded Him constantly. (*Jesus down; Peter up*)

Peter: We'll only let the most important people talk to Jesus. That way He won't get so tired. (*Peter down*)

Narrator: One day Jesus was busy teaching the people and healing the sick. Some mothers and fathers heard He was near. (*Mothers #1 and #2 up*)

Mother #1: Did you hear that Jesus is just outside town? Oh, I wish I could take my little Ruth to see Him. He is so kind and gentle.

Mother #2: I know. It would be so wonderful to have Jesus bless my baby.

Mother #1: Why don't we do it?

Mother #2: Do what?

Mother #1: Take our children to Jesus and ask Him to pray for them.

Mother #2: Do you think He would? (*Father up*)

Father: Who would do what?

Mother #1: We want to take our children to Jesus and ask Him to bless them.

Father: That sounds like a great idea. My son Obed has no grandfather to lay his hands on him and pray for him. Maybe Jesus would do that for him.

Narrator: Off the parents went in search of Jesus. They were eager to have Him bless their children. (*Add hillside*) But when they got to where Jesus was teaching, they got a disappointment.

Mother #1: Oh, dear. There are so many people that I can't see Jesus. How will Ruth ever be able to see Him?

Mother #2: I'll never get through that crowd with my baby.

Father: Let me see what I can do. Excuse me. Pardon me, could we please get through so our children can see Jesus?

Narrator: But the people were unwilling to let them through. The children tried to wriggle through small openings. Their parents followed as best they could, but they didn't get very far. Suddenly they came face to face with one of Jesus' followers. (*Peter up*)

Peter: Wait a minute there! Where do you think you are going?

Father: We brought our children to Jesus so He can put His hands on them and pray for them.

Peter: Children! Jesus has no time for children! He's far too busy and important to be bothered by babies and children.

Mother #1: But we wouldn't take much of His time.

Mother #2: If He would just hold my baby for a minute, then...

Peter: Go away! Stop bringing your children to Jesus. Don't annoy Him anymore.

Narrator: Unexpectedly, someone called out. *(Jesus up)*

Jesus: Wait! Let the little children come to me. Don't stop them.

Narrator: The mothers and fathers could hardly believe their ears.

Father: It is Jesus.

Mother #1: He is calling our children to come to Him.

Narrator: The people began to move aside as the parents and children stepped forward. At first the children held tightly to their parents' hands in fear. When they saw Jesus looking at them in love, they let go and began to run to Him. Jesus smiled and lifted the children onto His lap.

Jesus: The kingdom of Heaven belongs to people who are like these children.

Narrator: The mothers and fathers stood near Jesus. He took the babies in His arms and held them close. Then Jesus looked at the crowd of people.

Jesus: The truth is that all of you must accept God's kingdom like a little child or you will never enter it. You must depend completely on God for the forgiveness of your sins just like these little ones depend on their parents for food and care.

Narrator: That was a wonderful day. The mothers and fathers never forgot how Jesus took time to bless their children. And the children never forgot how Jesus held them

and prayed for them. Yes, Jesus always has time for children. He has time to love you today too.

Jesus and the Children

(tune: "Away in a Manger")

Away on a hillside, one bright summer's day,
Jesus was teaching the people to pray.
Mothers brought children for Jesus to bless,
His followers said, "Go away, stop such foolishness."

Then Jesus rebuked His disciples and said,
"Let the children come to me, and don't be mislead.
For theirs is the kingdom of Heaven, you see."
And He blessed them and touched them which made them happy.

Jesus Blesses the Children

On a day when Jesus was teaching,
   (Palms up, extend hands to indicate holding Bible.)
The people brought children to Him.
   (Hold up all fingers.)
"Go away and leave Jesus alone!"
   (Point away from self.)
The disciples faces were grim.
   (Angry look on faces.)
When Jesus saw this He said,
   (Place hand above eyes.)
"Let little ones come to me.
   (Beckon toward self.)
For theirs is the kingdom of Heaven,
   (Point upward.)
And you like them must be."
   (Point to others.)
Then Jesus took the children
   (Hold up five fingers.)
And blessed them all that day.
   (Hold up five more fingers.)
He hugged them and He kissed them
   (Cross arms over heart.)
And sent them on their way.
   (Wave good-bye.)

Up a Tree

Luke 19:1-10

(Jesus, Zacchaeus, Andrew, Man, Woman)

Jesus (*ring*)
Use from story "Rise and Shine."

Zacchaeus (*pinky*)
1   1 1/2" black pom
2   5 MM eyes
face #13
flesh, green felt; striped material
jewelry filigree
polyester stuffing
1 1/2" velcro
Attach belt #1 to robe and trim with filigree on chest. Gather hat crown #1 where shown. Stuff lightly with polyester to round out as if head is inside. Glue to top of pom. Fasten hatband #1 around head being sure to fasten to hat crown and pom.

Andrew (*thumb*)
Use from story "The More the Merrier."

Man (*middle*)

1   1 1/2" gold pom
2   5 MM eyes
face #16
flesh, dark green, peach felt
2" velcro
Glue belt #1 to robe. Attach headband around head pom.

Woman (*pointer*)
1   1 1/2" yellow pom
2   5 MM eyes
face #6
flesh, blue, white felt; striped material
1/4" blue ribbon
1 3/4" velcro
Fasten belt #1 to robe. Fold and glue head-scarf #2 around face. Add ribbon headband. Blush the cheeks.

Tree (*hand*)
green, brown felt
2" velcro
Attach tree top #1 to trunk #1. Glue this combined tree front to a plain piece of felt for backing. Trim this backing same shape as front.

Puppet Play

Narrator: Jesus was traveling through the city of Jericho. A man named Zacchaeus (*Zacchaeus up*) lived in Jericho. Now Zacchaeus was a tax collector. He was very rich and very, very important. But he got his riches by cheating people when he collected their taxes. You can imagine how that made people feel about him. They *hated* Zacchaeus! So although Zacchaeus had lots of money, a beautiful home, and many servants, he didn't have any friends.

Then he heard that Jesus was going through Jericho.

Zacchaeus: I want to see who this Jesus is. I've heard a lot about Him, but I want to see Him for myself. I'll go down to the highway and see Him.

Narrator: But when Zacchaeus got to the highway, there were people everywhere. *(Man and Woman up)* He jumped up and down trying to peek out between the people. But he was so short that all he could see were robes, and arms and the backs of people.

Zacchaeus: Can I get through here? Let me through.

Man: Quit shoving!

Zacchaeus: But I can't see the road.

Man: Well, I'm standing here and you can't get in front of me.

Woman: The nerve of that Zacchaeus! It's bad enough that he cheats us. Now he wants the best place in the crowd. Humph!

Narrator: Well, you can be very sure that *nobody* let Zacchaeus get in front of them to see Jesus!

Zacchaeus: I'll never get to see Jesus this way. I know—there's a big tree a little way down the road. If I climb up in it, I should be able to see everything that goes on. Jesus will be sure to pass under the tree. *(Add tree)*

Narrator: So Zacchaeus ran ahead to where a huge old tree stood right beside the highway. He got one foot up on a lower branch and then, umph! He got the other foot up and...pullllled himself onto a big limb that hung out over the road. And just in time too, for Jesus was coming straight towards him. *(Jesus and Andrew up)* Jesus and His followers walked along the highway. Closer and closer they came until...Wait! They stopped right under the tree Zacchaeus was sitting in. Jesus looked right up into the tree. He looked straight at Zacchaeus.

Jesus: Zacchaeus, hurry and come down! I'm going to have dinner at your house today.

Narrator: Zacchaeus' eyes boggled and he gulped. Jesus wanted to stay at his house. Why Jesus had actually *invited* himself to dinner at Zacchaeus' house! Would he come down? Zacchaeus almost fell down. He scrambled down as fast as his short, bowlegs would move. He bowed in front of Jesus.

Woman: Oh, my. Look at the kind of man Jesus stays with!

Man: Zacchaeus is a tax collector—a terrible sinner!

Andrew: Are You sure You want to stay at this man's house, Lord?

Jesus: Yes, I am sure. I, the Son of Man, came to find lost people like Zacchaeus and save them.

Zacchaeus: Right this way, Lord. Follow me.

Narrator: The crowd followed Jesus to Zacchaeus' house. Only Jesus' followers went inside the house with Him. The people stood outside and complained.

Man: I can't imagine why Jesus would want to eat with someone like Zacchaeus.

Woman: Jesus even treated him like a friend!

Narrator: Zacchaeus was delighted to be able to talk face to face with Jesus. We don't know what they talked about that day, but whatever it was, it changed Zacchaeus' life. He had found a friend. When Jesus left his house, Zacchaeus spoke to Him loudly so all the people around could hear him.

Zacchaeus: Lord, I will give half of my money to the poor. If I have cheated anyone...

Man: If? There is no if about it. He *has* cheated—everyone!

Zacchaeus: If I have cheated anyone, I will pay that person back four times more than I took.

Woman: I hear it, but I don't believe it.

Jesus: Salvation has come to this house today.

Zacchaeus: I want to do whatever You ask me to do, Lord.

Jesus: Zacchaeus, because you are sorry for your sin and want to make things right, you now belong to God's family.

Narrator: Zacchaeus was true to his word. He gave half of his money to the poor in Jericho. He paid back everyone he had cheated four times more than he had taken. And after that day with Jesus, he collected only the money that the government demanded. The people of Jericho no longer hated Zacchaeus. They were glad to be his friends. When we confess our sins to Jesus and receive His forgiveness, our lives will also be different. Like Zacchaeus, we will belong to God's family.

Zacchaeus Climbed a Tree

(tune: "Farmer in the Dell")

Zacchaeus climbed a tree,
Zacchaeus climbed a tree,

Because Jesus he couldn't see,
He climbed it carefully.

Jesus called out to him,
Jesus called out to him,
"I must stay at your house today,
So come down from that limb."

Jesus and Zacchaeus

When Jesus came to Jericho,
    (Move fingers in palm of other hand to indicate walking.)
Zacchaeus climbed a tree;
    (Move arms upward to indicate climbing.)
For great was the crowd of people that day,
    (Hold up all fingers.)
And he was too short to see.
    (Crouch down.)
But Jesus saw him up in the tree,
    (Place hand above eyes.)
And saw in his heart also.
    (Place hand over heart.)
"Come down here, Zacchaeus," Jesus said.
    (Beckon towards self.)
"For it's to your house I'll go."
    (Touch fingertips of both hands together in indicate roof.)
Zacchaeus changed from bad to good
When Jesus entered in.
    (Place hand over heart.)
And my life too will change to good
    (Point to self.)
When Jesus forgives my sin.
    (Fold hands; bow head.)

Monarch of All He Surveys

John 20:1-18

(Jesus, Mary Magdalene, Peter, John, 2 Angels)

Jesus (thumb)
Use from story, "Rise and Shine."

Mary Magdalene (pointer)
1 1 1/2" brown pom
2 5 MM eyes
face #7
flesh, orange felt; striped material
2" velcro
Use striped material on a diagonal for belt #1 and headscarf #2. Attach belt to robe. Attach one end of headscarf to side of face. Wrap around head and secure scarf at other side of face and over shoulder. Blush the cheeks.

Peter (middle)
Use from story "Children Should Be Seen and Not Heard."

John (ring)
1 1 1/2" red-brown pom

2 5 MM eyes
face #16
flesh, light blue, light orange felt
2" velcro
Fasten coat #2 to robe. Attach headband around head pom.

Angels (pinky)
2 1 1/2" yellow poms
4 5 MM eyes
faces #10
flesh, yellow felt
2 1" velcro
Attach faces low on pom so no hair shows for beard.

Tomb (hand)
Use tomb and stone from story "A Matter of Life and Death."

Puppet Play

Narrator: It had been a terrible day. Jesus was dead. Two of His friends had buried Jesus in a rock tomb in a beautiful garden. (Add tomb with stone covering the doorway) Jesus' enemies had gotten permission to have Roman soldiers guard the tomb so nobody could take away Jesus' body. Mary Magdalene (Mary up) had a big lump in her throat and an empty place in her heart. Her best friend, Jesus, was dead.

Mary Magdalene: If only there was something I could do for Jesus. I know, I can take some sweet smelling spices to pour on His body. It isn't much, but maybe it will show God how much I loved His Son.

Narrator: So Mary took the spices and hurried out to the garden where Jesus was buried. It was very early in the morning and still dark. The sun wouldn't come up for several hours.

Mary Magdalene: I wonder if one of the soldiers will help me roll away the stone from the tomb? It is so heavy that I can't do it by myself.

Narrator: Mary entered the garden. She looked for the soldiers who had been guarding the grave. But they were not there. *(Remove stone from tomb.)*

Mary Magdalene: Here is the fire they built to warm themselves, but the soldiers are gone. Now what shall I do about the stone? Wait! The stone has been rolled away from the tomb! What has happened? Has someone stolen the Lord's body? Oh, I must tell Peter and John about this!

Narrator: Mary ran as fast as she could to find the two men. *(Peter and John up)* She was out of breath when she found them.

Mary Magdalene: Peter. John. They have taken...the Lord...out of the tomb. I don't know...where they have...put Him!

Peter: Come on, John. Let's go see.

Narrator: Peter and John were excited. They raced to the garden. John ran faster and he beat Peter to the tomb. He bent down and looked in.

John: The cloth strips are there, but the body is gone.

Narrator: Peter went into the tomb.

Peter: Yes, the cloth strips are here. And over there is the cloth that was folded around Jesus' head. Look, John. That cloth is folded up and laying in a different place from the rest of the cloth strips.

Narrator: John followed Peter into the tomb.

John: Jesus is alive again! Jesus is alive!

Peter: I don't know, John. It sounds like nonsense. Why, it's impossible!

John: Then how do you explain this?

Peter: I don't know what this means. Let's go back home. I want to think about all of this. *(Peter and John down)*

Narrator: After the men left, Mary stood outside the tomb, crying. She bent down and looked inside the tomb. What a surprise she had! The tears in her eyes made everything blurry, but there, right in front of her, were two angels sitting where Jesus' body had been. One angel sat at the head and one at the foot. *(Angels up)*

Angels: Why are you crying?

Mary Magdalene: Someone has taken Jesus away. I don't know where they have put Him.

Narrator: Suddenly, Mary felt someone standing behind her. The sun was just beginning to send pink and gold fingers into the black night sky. It was hard to see who was standing there. Mary thought it was the gardener. *(Angels down; Jesus up)*

Jesus: Why are you crying? Are you looking for someone?

Mary Magdalene: Did you take Jesus away? If you did, Sir, please tell me where you have put Him. I'll go get Him and take Him away.

Jesus: Mary.

Narrator: The man's voice was soft and loving. Mary knew at once who He was.

Mary Magdalene: Teacher, Jesus!

Narrator: She knelt before Jesus.

Jesus: Don't delay me. I haven't gone up to

the Father yet. Go and tell my followers that I am going back to my God and your God; My heavenly Father and your heavenly Father. *(Jesus down)*

Narrator: Suddenly, Jesus disappeared! The sun peeked over the tops of the trees and painted the dewdrops on the flowers a soft pink color. Birds woke up. They began to sing their spring songs. Mary jumped to her feet. The lump was gone from her throat and the empty place in her heart was filled with joy. She ran to find Jesus' followers. With every step she took, her mind was singing, "He's alive, Jesus is alive!" And that was the first Easter morning!

Easter Joy

(tune: "It's Bubbling in My Soul")

He's alive, He's alive,
Jesus rose up from the dead.

There's singing, and laughing,
Since Jesus lives again.

Folks don't understand it,
Nor can they keep it quiet,

For Jesus Christ, the Lord of all,
Has changed death into life.

Jesus Lives Again

Very early on that day,
Mary walked along the way.
(Move fingers in palm of other hand to indicate walking.)
To Jesus' tomb she hurried on
(Move fingers quickly in palm of other hand to indicate running.)
And there she found the stone was gone.
(Form a circle with hands to indicate the tomb's opening)
Quickly she ran to tell Peter and John
(Hold up two fingers.)
"They took Jesus away. His body is gone!"
(Cup hands around mouth).
They ran to the tomb and found it was true.
(Nod head.)
Then the men went home. They were feeling blue.
(Hang head; look sad.)
Mary bent down and looked in the tomb.
(Bend down; place hand above eyes.)
Two angels sat there, lighting up the gloom.
(Cup hands around face.)
Then Mary turned 'round and saw Jesus outside.
(Turn around in place.)
"Mary," He called, "I'm alive though I died."
(Cup hands around mouth.)
Mary Magdalene left and told the rest,
(Hold up all fingers.)
"I saw the Lord! I've truly been blest."
(Point to self; smile.)

73

A Stitch in Time

Acts 9:36-42

(Peter, Tabitha, Widow, Mother, Child)

Peter (thumb)
Use from story, "Monarch of All He Surveys."

Tabitha (pointer)
1   1 1/2" brown pom
2   5 MM eyes
face #6
tan, rose, white felt
fancy braid, narrow braid
1 1/2" velcro
Glue yoke #3 to robe and add trim to yoke and bottom of robe. Attach belt of narrow braid. Fasten braid headband around head pom. Blush the cheeks.

Widow (ring)
1   1 1/2" gray pom
2   5 MM eyes
face #11
tan, lavender felt; striped material
2" velcro

Attach belt #1 to robe. Fold and glue headband #2 around face. Blush the cheeks.

Mother and Child (middle)
Use mother and child #1 from story "Children Should Be Seen and Not Heard."

Child #2 (pinky)
1   1" yellow pom
2   4 MM eyes
face #12
flesh, blue felt; striped material
1/4" blue ribbon
1 1/2" velcro
Attach coat #3 to robe. Glue ribbon headband around head pom.

House (hand)
Use from story, "Blessing in Disguise."

Puppet Play

Narrator: Tabitha lived in Joppa. (*Tabitha up*) She was a follower of Jesus and was always very busy doing things for other people. (*Mother up*)

Tabitha: Here is a new robe for your little girl.

Mother: Oh, thank you, Tabitha. It is so hard finding enough money to buy cloth to make clothes for all my children. What would we do without you? (*Mother down; widow up*)

Tabitha: I swept the floor and brought fresh water for you, Miriam.

Widow: Thank you, Tabitha. You have been so helpful since I have been sick. (*Widow down; child #2 up*)

Tabitha: Jared, I think you must have grown three inches since I made you that coat last spring. It's time you had a new one.

Child: You've been like a mother to me ever since my own mother died, Tabitha. Father and I are so thankful to the Lord for you. *(child down)*

Narrator: Now Peter was visiting in Lydda which was a town near Joppa. While he was there, Tabitha became very sick and died. *(Tabitha down)* The people of Joppa were heartbroken. *(Mother, widow, child up)* They prepared Tabitha's body for burial and placed it in the upstairs room of her house. *(Add house)*

Mother: How will we ever get along without Tabitha?

Widow: Who will help me now? I'm too old and sick to take care of myself.

Child: Did you hear that Peter healed Aeneas in Lydda? Now Aeneas can walk.

Widow: Yes, Aeneas hadn't been able to get out of his bed for the past eight years! He was worse off than I am.

Mother: I'm happy for Aeneas. But what has that got to do with Tabitha's death?

Child: We could ask Peter to come. Maybe he could make Tabitha well again.

Mother: Do you think Peter could do that?

Child: I think he could!

Widow: It wouldn't hurt to ask him.

Mother: Then let's send somebody to ask Peter to help us.

Widow: Who can we send?

Child: My father could go.

Mother: My husband could go with him. Let's hurry and ask them to do it right away.

Narrator: So the two men went to find Peter. *(Peter up)* "Hurry, and please come with us!" they said. Peter hastened back to Joppa with the men. When They got to Tabitha's house, they took Peter to the upstairs room where they had laid her body. Everybody she had helped stood around crying.

Mother: My little Deborah is wearing the new robe Tabitha made for her.

Child: Tabitha made this coat for me just a week ago.

Narrator: Peter could see that the people were very sad. They all loved kind Tabitha very much and didn't know how they could get along without her. Peter's own heart was touched with sympathy for them. He knew what Jesus would do.

Peter: Everybody leave the room.

Narrator: After the people had gone out, Peter knelt down and prayed. Then he turned and spoke to the body.

Peter: Tabitha, stand up.

Narrator: Tabitha's pale cheeks turned pink again. Her eyelids fluttered. Then she opened her eyes. When she saw Peter, she sat up. *(Tabitha up)*

Peter: Here, Tabitha, take my hand. I will help you up. Friends, you may come in. Tabitha is alive!

Narrator: The people were overjoyed to see their dear friend alive again. The news spread quickly throughout the city. Many people believed in the Lord because of this miracle. And what happened to Tabitha? She continued helping people as she had before. What a wonderful way to show her love for the Lord Jesus. And we can show our love for Him by helping others too!

Peter and Tabitha

(tune: "Row, Row, Row Your Boat")

Sew, sew, sew a coat
For those who were in need;
Sew a robe and help the poor;
She was a friend indeed.
Cry, cry, cry they did,
When Tabitha was dead.
But Peter came and raised her up,
And praise to God did spread.

Peter Raises Tabitha to Life

Tabitha lived in Joppa town.
   (Touch fingertips of both hands together to indicate roof.)
There she helped the poor.
   (Extend hands.)
Sewing coats and shirts for all
   (Move thumb and pointer finger together to indicate sewing.)
The needy around her door.
   (Extend arms to sides.)
While Peter visited a town nearby,
   (Touch fingertips of both hands together to indicate roof.)
Tabitha grew sick and died.
   (Lay head on hands.)
Jesus' followers sent for Peter to come.
   (Move fingers in palm of other hand to indicate walking.)
"Please help us," they cried.
   (Beckon toward self.)
When Peter saw the good she had done,
   (Point to eyes.)
He bowed his knees and prayed.
   (Fold hands; bow head.)
"Stand up," he said and she sat up.
   (Raise arms.)
Then praises to God were made.
   (Point upward.)

By Word of Mouth

Acts 16:16-34

(Paul, Silas, Jailer, Prisoners #1 and #2, Wife, Child)

Paul *(pointer)*
1 1 1/2" black pom
2 5 MM eyes
face #2
flesh, dark yellow, blue felt; striped material
2" velcro
Glue belt #1 to robe. Attach coat #1 to robe. Attach headband around pom.

Silas *(middle)*
1 1 1/2" brown pom
2 5 MM eyes
face #3
flesh, green felt; striped material
narrow white braid
2" velcro
Glue coat #2 to robe. Add braid trim to coat. Attach headband around pom.

Jailer *(ring)*
1 1 1/2" black pom
2 5 MM eyes

face #3
flesh, orange, brown, gray felt
2" velcro
Attach #1 hands to front sleeves of robe #2. Glue belt #2 to robe and add sword. Fasten one hand to robe and other hand to top of sword #3.

Prisoner #1 *(thumb)*
1 1 1/2" red-brown pom
2 5 MM eyes
face #15
flesh, red-brown felt
1" velcro
Glue strands of hair over forehead.

Prisoner #2 *(thumb)*
1 1 1/2" white pom
2 5 MM eyes
face #15
flesh, white, dark blue felt
1" velcro
Fasten headband around head pom.

Wife *(pinky)*
1 1 1/2" yellow pom
2 5 MM eyes
face #5
flesh, yellow felt; striped material
1" velcro
Glue face low on pom. Wrap headscarf #2 around head pom and under chin. Trim away excess scarf. Blush the cheeks.

Child *(pinky)*
1 1" brown pom
2 4 MM eyes
face #12
flesh, brown felt
1" velcro
Fasten face low on pom. Glue strands of hair over forehead.

Jail *(hand)*
    gray, felt
    2" velcro
    Cut two pieces from jail pattern. Add details to front with marker. Glue to back.

Puppet Play

Narrator: The soldiers dragged their prisoners, Paul and Silas, down the streets of Philippi. *(Paul and Silas up)* The prisoner's backs were cut and bleeding but the soldiers didn't care. They had even joined the crowd of angry people who beat Paul and Silas. Now the soldiers were taking them to jail. When the jailer saw them, he quickly opened the door. *(Jailer up)* "Here," growled one of the soldiers as he pushed them into a cell. *(Add jail)* "Be sure to guard these men very carefully."

Jailer: You can be sure they won't get away. I'll chain their hands to the walls and fasten their feet between these large blocks of wood. Now there's no way they can escape!

Narrator: The heavy wooden door swung shut and the iron lock was fastened tightly. The hollow sounds of the jailer's footsteps on the stone floor grew fainter. *(Jailer down)* Paul and Silas were alone in the cold, damp room. Alone? Well, not exactly alone. There were rats that skittered across the room, their claws scratching on the stones. And huge black spiders sat in their webs staring at these new intruders. Cockroaches ran races up and down the walls and floor. Down the hall, a prisoner called out through the darkness. *(Prisoners #1 and #2 up)*

Prisoner #1: What crime did you two do?

Paul: We drove an evil spirit out of a young servant girl by using the name of Jesus, the Christ.

Prisoner #2: And they put you in the most secure cell for that? Why?

Silas: Because her owners could no longer make money by her telling fortunes.

Prisoner #1: If they treated me like they did you, I would be very angry.

Narrator: But Paul and Silas were not angry. Hurting, hungry, cold, mistreated, locked up in a dreadful cell, they did the most amazing thing of all. About midnight Paul and Silas were praying and singing songs to God. The other prisoners were listening to them.

Prisoner #2: Did you hear those two prisoners praying?

Prisoner #1: Yes. They were praying for that servant girl they helped. Then they prayed for the very men who had them arrested and beaten. Now they are singing. I think they are crazy.

Prisoner #2: I can't understand how they can sing in this place! What are they singing about?

Prisoner #1: Some kind of praises to their God. Did you feel that? It felt like an earthquake.

Prisoner #2: EARTHQUAKE! Help! The floor is shaking and the walls are cracking.

Narrator: Paul and Silas' chains snapped from the wall. The boards holding their feet twisted apart. The heavy wooden door creaked and groaned. Then it lurched off its hinges and fell out into the hall with a crash. In other cells the same things were happening. The jailer leaped to his feet and lunged down the hall toward the cells. *(Jailer up)* He tripped on a door and fell to his knees. His worst nightmare had come true.

Jailer: All the doors of the jail are open. The prisoners are free. By now they have all escaped. I cannot face torture by the authorities for letting this happen. I will kill myself.

Narrator: He reached for the short sword he carried. Just then Paul shouted.

Paul: Don't hurt yourself! Nobody has escaped. We are all here!

Jailer: Bring me a light.

Narrator: Soon the jailer was inside the cell. He was shaking with fear and fell down before Paul and Silas.

Jailer: You are not criminals. You are good men. Your God has done this. What must I do to be saved?

Paul: Believe in the Lord Jesus and you will be saved.

Silas: You and all the people in your house can become the children of God.

Jailer: Come home with me and tell us all about this Jesus. *(Prisoner #1 and #2 down; remove jail)*

Narrator: So Paul and Silas told the jailer and all the people in his house about the Lord. *(Wife and child up)* The jailer washed Paul and Silas' wounds and his wife helped bandage them with clean cloths. Then the jailer and all his people were baptized.

Wife: Here, have some cheese and olives. Son, bring the grapes and figs for our guests.

Child: Father, do we really belong to God's family now that we believe in Jesus?

Jailer: Yes, my child. And all because God answered Paul and Silas' prayers in jail.

Narrator: What a happy day it was for that family in Philippi. And it was only the beginning of a friendship between the people there and Paul. Paul never forgot Jesus' followers in Philippi.

Paul and Silas Praise God

(tune: "Old MacDonald Had a Farm")

God sent an earthquake to the jail
Where Paul and Silas were.
He set them free and saved the jailer
Where Paul and Silas were.
Now they all praise God
And thank the Lord.
Giving glory, singing praise,
Telling others of their joy.
Because Paul and Silas were in jail
Singing songs to God.

Paul and Silas in Jail

Paul and Silas were thrown in jail.
  (Place two fingers in palm of other hand; close hand around them.)
They trusted in God; He would not fail.
  (Shake head.)
Songs of praise filled the jail that night.
  (Fold hands; bow head.)
And God sent an earthquake of power and might.
  (Flex arm to show muscle.)
It freed the two men and frightened the jailer.
  (Look frightened.)
His knees were shaking and his face grew paler.
  (Shake body.)
With trembling hand, he reached for his spear.
  (Extend hand.)
But Paul shouted loudly, "We are all here."
  (Cup hands around mouth.)
The jailer and his family were saved that night.
  (Hold up all fingers.)
They trusted the Lord Jesus and rejoiced in His might.
  (Point upward.)

It's No Secret

Acts 23:11-35

(Paul, Nephew, Soldier, Commander, Jews #1 and #2)

Paul *(middle)*
Use from story "By Word of Mouth."

Nephew *(pointer)*
1 1" black pom
2 4 MM eyes
face #9; child body
flesh, orange, green felt
1 1/2" velcro
Attach coat #3 to robe. Fasten headband around head pom.

Soldier *(thumb)*
1 1 1/2" brown pom
2 5 MM eyes
face #6
flesh, red, gold felt
1 1/2" velcro
Roman soldiers were clean shaven and had a specific uniform. Attach armor #2 to red robe. Glue armor #4 to each shoulder.

Fasten armor #6 to robe and glue belt #5 over it at the top. Add details with marker.

Commander *(ring)*
1 1 1/2" black pom
2 5 MM eyes
face #5
flesh, red, gold felt
2" velcro
Fasten armor #5 over robe. Attach armor #3 to robe and add armor #1 to each shoulder. Glue on belt #5. Add drape #4 to left shoulder and cloak #2 to back of robe. Add details with marker.

Jew #1 *(pinky)*
1 1 1/2" gold pom
2 5 MM eyes
face #13
flesh, gold, blue-green felt
1" velcro
Gather hat crown #1 where shown. Stuff lightly with polyester to round out as if head is inside. Glue to top of pom. Fasten hatband #1 around head being sure to fasten to hat crown and pom.

Jew #2 *(pinky))*
1 1 1/2" white pom
2 5 MM eyes
face #15
flesh, white, gold felt
1" velcro
Fasten headband around head pom.

Castle of Antonia *(hand)*
gray felt
2" velcro
Cut 2 pieces of castle pattern. Add details to front with marker. Glue to back piece.

Puppet Play

Narrator: Nathan stood motionless in a corner of the outer court of the temple. *(Nephew up)* Had he really heard what he thought he heard? He ducked back into the shadow of the pillar. The men were still talking in low voices. *(Jews #1 and #2 up)*

Jew #1: I will ask the commander to bring Paul out to me. I'll tell him I want to ask Paul more questions. You will be waiting to kill him while he is on the way here.

Jew #2: Right. And remember, we have made a promise not to eat or drink until we have killed Paul!

Narrator: Nathan's knees were shaking. There was a big lump in his throat. These men weren't just talking about any Paul. They were talking about his Uncle Paul. And he had just heard them plan to kill him! Nathan tried to look casual as he walked out of the courtyard. *(Jews #1 and #2 down)* As soon as he reached the street, he started running in the direction of the army building, the Castle of Antonia. *(Add castle)* Only a few days before, he had watched his Uncle Paul being taken there as a prisoner by Roman soldiers. Now he raced up the steps and through the gateway. He had to tell Uncle Paul what he had heard! *(Soldier up)*

Soldier: Halt! Where do you think you are going, Boy?

Nathan: Please, Sir. I have an important message for the prisoner Paul. *(Soldier down)*

Narrator: Soon Nathan was standing in front of his uncle *(Paul up)* telling him the whole story.

Nathan: Oh, Uncle Paul. Our whole family has been praying that God would deliver you from jail by an angel or an earthquake or something. And now these men are planning to killing you!

Paul: It will be all right. Last night the Lord came and stood by me. He told me that I must tell people in Rome about Him just as I have told the people here in Jerusalem. He has allowed you to overhear this secret plan. I believe that you, Nathan, are the one the Lord will use to get me to Rome. Now, you must do something more for me. Can you be very brave?

Nathan: I will try to be brave, Uncle Paul.

Paul: Good. Now here's what I want you to do.

Narrator: Paul whispered his plan to Nathan. Then he called the soldier to him. *(Soldier up)*

Paul: Take this young man to the commander. He has a message for him. And Nathan...

Nathan: Yes, Uncle Paul?

Paul: Be brave.

Narrator: Nathan's knees were shaking so badly that he could hardly stand in front of the commander. *(Commander up)* His hands were icy and he felt feverish. The commander saw how frightened he was.

Commander: Come over here where we can be alone. *(Soldier down)* Now, what do you want to tell me?

Narrator: Nathan told the commander what he had heard in the temple.

Nathan: Please, Sir. Don't believe the Jews. There are more than forty of them who are hiding and waiting to kill Paul!

Commander: I will take care of this matter. Captain! *(Soldier up)* Get two hundred soldiers ready to go to Caesarea tonight. Also, get seventy horsemen and two hundred men with spears. They must be ready to leave at nine o'clock. Oh, yes, get a horse ready for Paul to ride. You will personally take him to the governor. *(Soldier down)* Now, young man, don't tell anyone that you have told me about this secret plan of the Jews. (*Commander down*)

Narrator: That night four hundred and seventy soldiers left the Castle of Antonia. And in the middle of all the soldiers, the apostle Paul rode safely away from the men who planned to murder him. And what about Paul's nephew? We don't know if his name really was Nathan because the Bible doesn't tell us the name of Paul's nephew. But we do know that the Lord used a little boy to deliver one of His greatest followers from jail and death. The Lord can use you, too, to help His followers in many ways. Will you be brave for the Lord? He has promised us, "I will never leave you." (Deuteronomy 31:6; Hebrews 13:5) You can depend on the Lord!

Paul's Brave Nephew

(tune: *"Jesus Loves Me"*)

Paul's young nephew heard a plan.
He knew it was evil and he ran
Straight to tell Paul what he'd heard,
Then he told him every word.
    Paul's nephew was brave,
    Paul's nephew was brave,
    Paul's nephew was brave,
And he trusted God.

I can trust God like this boy
Helping evil to destroy.
Depend on God to guide me right;
Wear His armor in the fight.
    Yes, I can be brave.
    Yes, I can be brave.
    Yes, I can be brave.
And I can trust God.

Paul's Nephew Helps Paul

The Jews hated Paul and made a plan
    (*Cup hands around mouth.*)
To trick the Romans and kill God's man.
Paul's young nephew heard their scheme.
    (*Cup hand around ears.*)
He ran to tell Paul, it was like a bad dream.
    (*Move fingers quickly in palm of other hand to indicate running.*)
God used the nephew to save Paul that day
    (*Hold up finger.*)
And sent along soldiers to guard his way.
    (*Wrap fingers of other hand around finger.*)
The boy went home very happy indeed.
    (*Use finger to draw a smile on face.*)
For God had used him to meet Paul's need.
    (*Point upward.*)
I can ask God to use me too;
    (*Fold hands; bow head.*)
Then go and help others like you and you.
    (*Point to others.*) child body

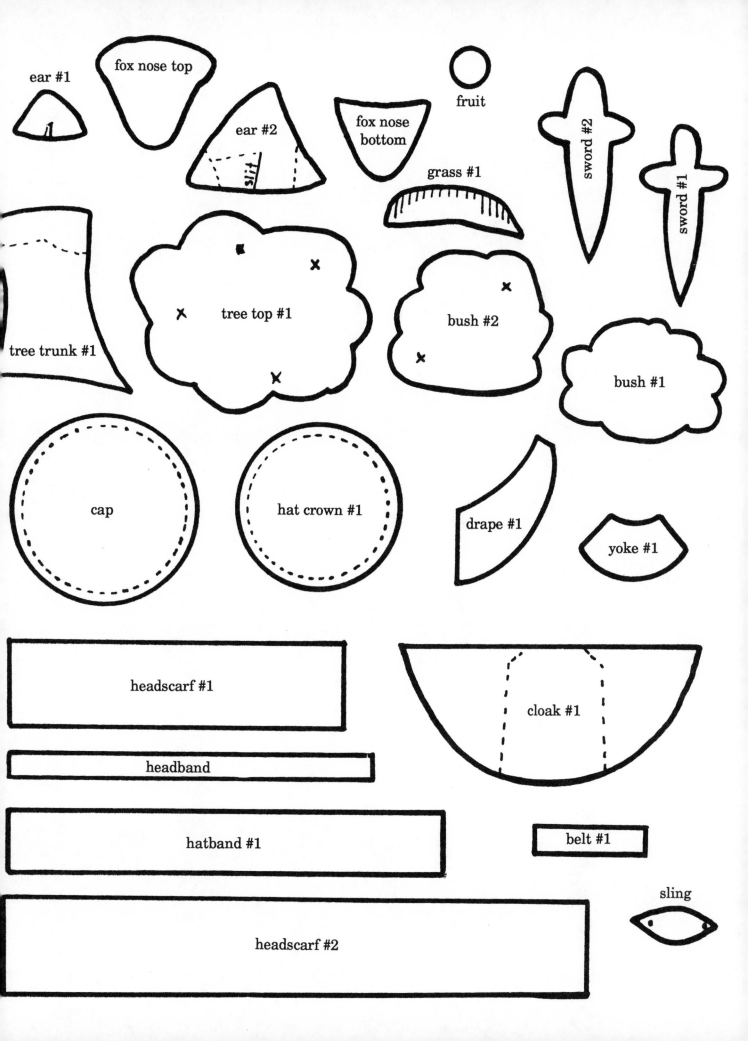

rabbit nose

ear #3

ear #4

axe

ear #5

monkey jaw

monkey face

ear #6

bow-blue

ark roof

bow-green

bow-yellow

bow-red

coat #2

rainbow back

tree top #2

ark back

ark

tree truck #2

baby blanket #1

grass #2

grass #3

grass #4

grass #5

water #1

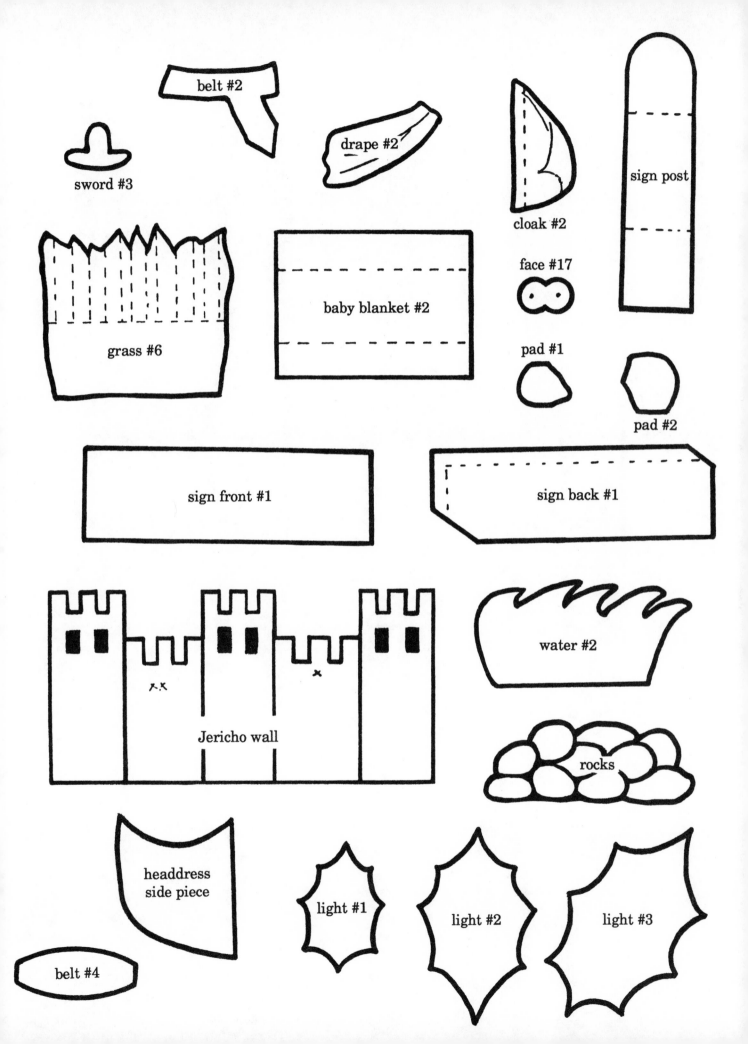

belt #2

drape #2

sword #3

cloak #2

sign post

face #17

baby blanket #2

pad #1

grass #6

pad #2

sign front #1

sign back #1

water #2

Jericho wall

rocks

headdress
side piece

light #1

light #2

light #3

belt #4

sash

armor

Goliath robe

ephod

oven

oven interior

stream

coals

yoke #2

breastplate

drape #3

belt #3

flame

flame

flame

hat crown #2

yoke #3

coat #3

lion nose #1

ear #7

lion nose #2

ear #8

hatband #2

lion

hay

baby blanket #3

manger

roof

stable front

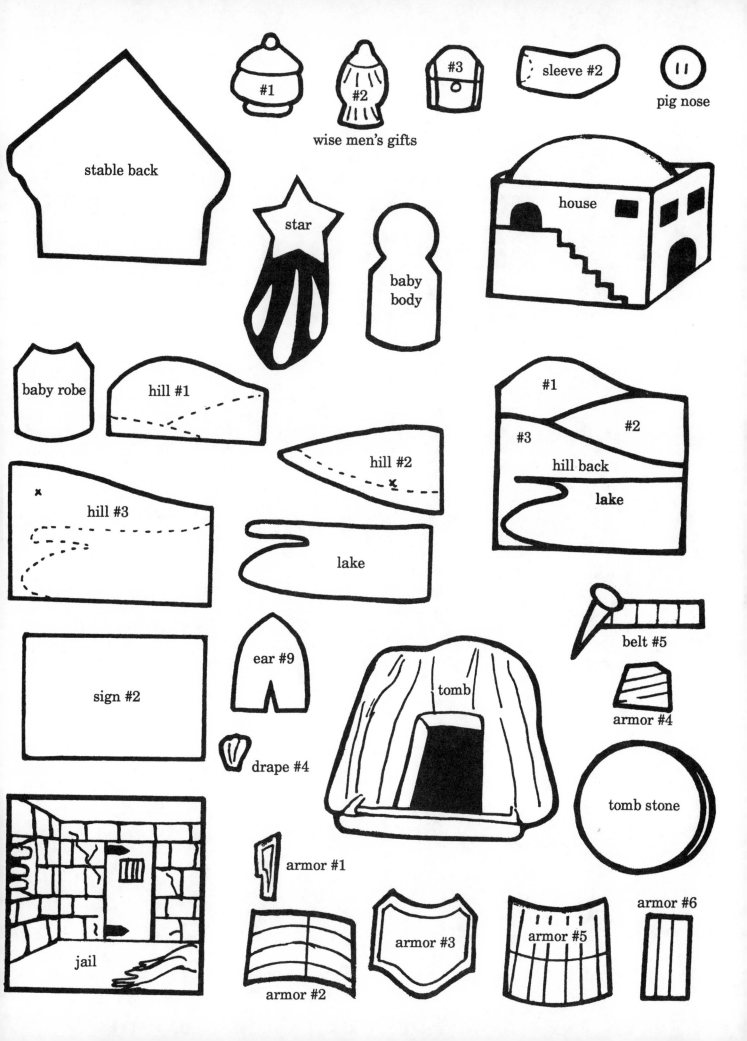

stable back

#1
#2
#3
sleeve #2
pig nose

wise men's gifts

star

baby body

house

baby robe

hill #1

#1

#2

#3

hill #2

hill back

lake

hill #3

lake

belt #5

sign #2

ear #9

tomb

armor #4

drape #4

tomb stone

armor #1

jail

armor #2

armor #3

armor #5

armor #6

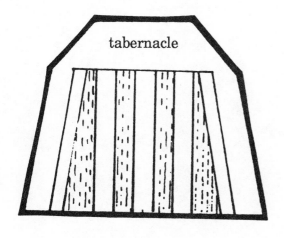
tabernacle

Castle of Antonia

palace

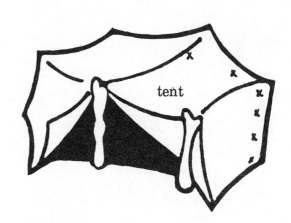
tent

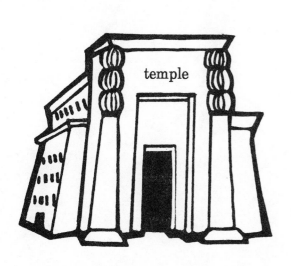
temple

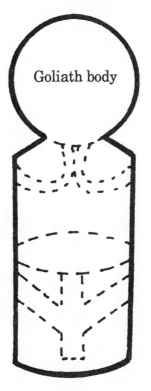
Goliath body

snake

bird